LONDON'S
THEATRICAL HERITAGE

DAVID C. RAMZAN

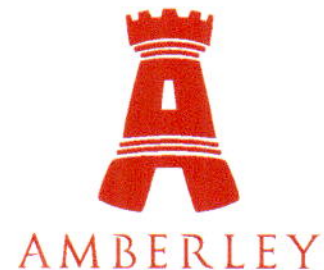

AMBERLEY

First published 2025

Amberley Publishing
The Hill, Stroud,
Gloucestershire, GL5 4EP

www.amberley-books.com

ISBN: 978 1 3981 2042 6 (print)
ISBN: 978 1 3981 2043 3 (ebook)

British Library Cataloguing in Publication Data.
A catalogue record for this book is available from the British Library.

Typeset in 10pt on 13pt Celeste.
Typesetting by Hurix Digital, India.
Printed in the UK.

EU GPSR Authorised Representative
Appointed EU Representative: Easy Access System Europe Oü, 16879218
Address: Mustamäe tee 50, 10621, Tallinn, Estonia
Contact Details: gpsr.requests@easproject.com, +358 40 500 3575

Contents

Introduction

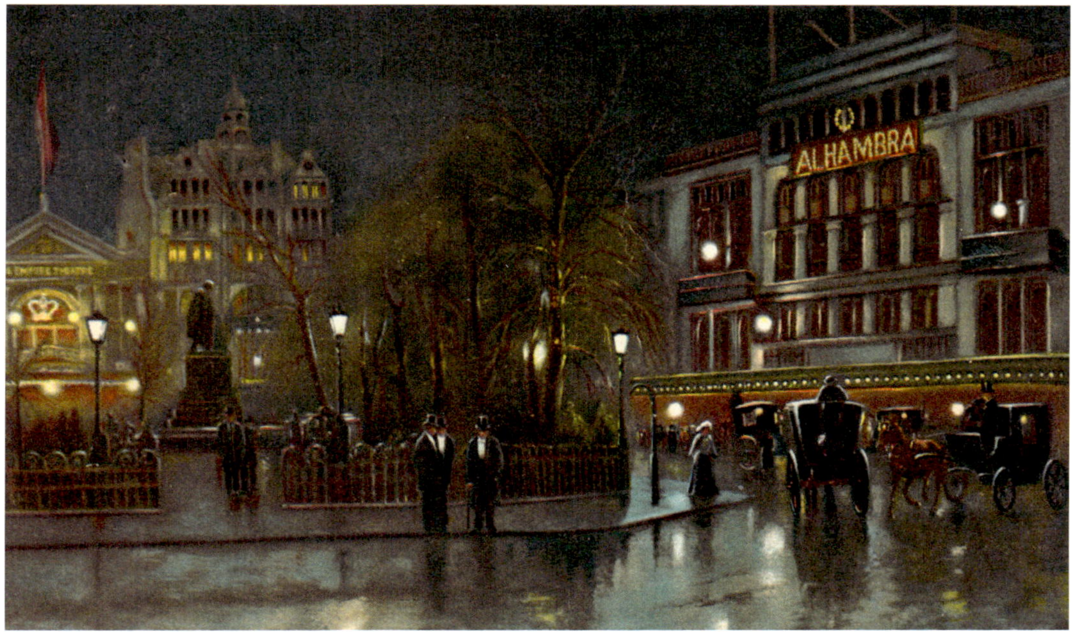

Leicester Square nightlife, 1900s.

In these modern times, a majority of London's theatres are located in the City of Westminster, an area known as the West End, and along the Strand and Shaftesbury Avenue, the capital's streets illuminated at night with their colourful, bright illuminations. Several other principal London theatres are also located within the ancient boundary of the City of London to the east, and south of the River Thames at Southwark, once part of Surrey.

All vicinities were incorporated within Greater London as a whole, which grew and evolved as a result of ceremonial and administration requirements, where many more theatres and performance spaces can be discovered throughout a majority of London's boroughs, many established and built before London spread outwards into the suburbs. London's 'theatreland' now has the most concentration of theatres than any other city around the globe.

London's theatrical heritage, however, first began within the City of London's boundary and can be traced back to a time after the Romans invaded Britain and established a *vicus*, an encampment, on the north bank of the River Thames, once an important river crossing point and territorial intersection for tribes of ancient Britons.

Before the arrival of the Romans, these ancient Britons would have taken part in their own cultural theatrical performances for ritualistic or religious ceremonies, in readiness for war, or acting out legends and stories from times past, many involving dance and song. These rituals were performed at places that had historical significance to early settlers, yet it would be the Romans who constructed London's first purpose-built theatre of entertainment.

1

Roman London's Theatrical Attraction

As the early Roman settlement evolved into an important riverside port and fortified town, known as Londinium, large splendid-looking properties were erected for the wealthiest of Roman London's citizens away from the quayside area of the city, where the poorer class of society resided in more modest houses erected amongst warehouses and stores, and *barracoons*, a place where slaves waited for transportation to other parts of Rome's empire. These slaves, many of whom were Britons captured during Roman occupation, were destined to become servants, fight as cohorts in Roman legions, or compete in gladiatorial exhibitions, a popular form of entertainment of the day.

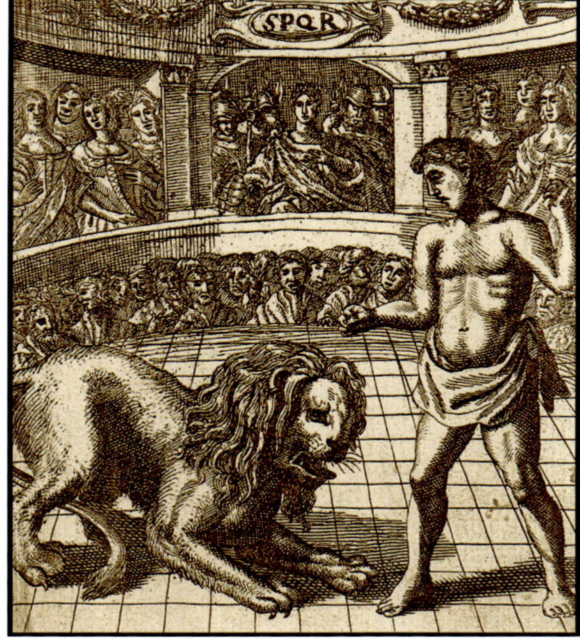

Roman citizens' entertainment: gladiator facing lion in the first century AD. (Wellcome Collection)

Gladiatorial combats, and the slaughter of wild beasts, took place within a purpose-built amphitheatre, or colosseum, and it has been speculated through the years by archaeologists and historical scholars that, like many Roman settlements which grew into large towns and cities, Londinium's development would have included the building of an amphitheatre.

It had been speculated London's Roman amphitheatre was erected close to the port area known as Queenhithe, opposite the reconstructed Tudor playhouse Shakespeare's Globe on the Southbank, while another suggestion was at Farringdon Street, near the River Fleet, where a large man-made mound was thought to have been part of an amphitheatre, situated outside the city's walls. It would have been a more common location for an amphitheatre, as a place of the execution and slaughter of men, women, and wild beasts would not have been permitted within the city wall. However, up until the mid-1900s, there had been no archaeological indication London ever had an amphitheatre.

When London suffered bombing raids during the Second World War, the Guildhall Art Gallery, to the south-east of the fifteenth-century Guildhall, the centre of civic government, was destroyed during one of those night raids. The site was left vacant up until 1987. A team of archaeologists then began excavating the site before construction work began on a new gallery where the remains of London's Roman amphitheatre were discovered. Surprisingly the amphitheatre was located within the city wall, the remnants consisting of two lengths of curved walls situated around a large sand and gravel arena.

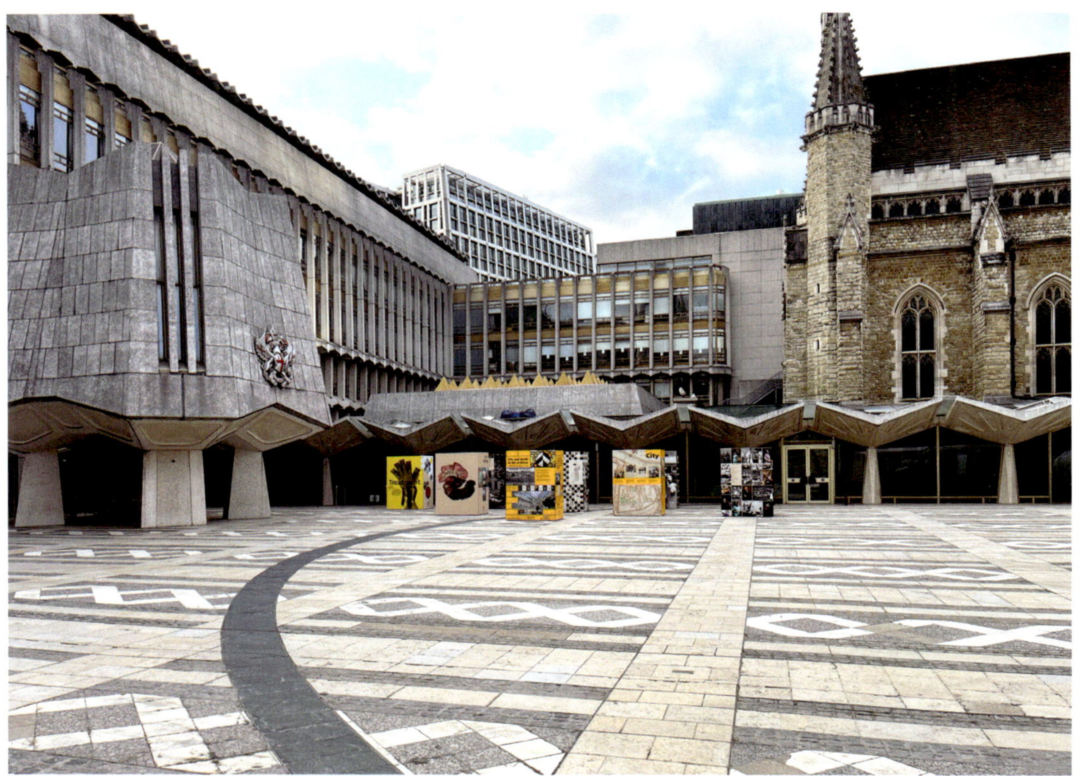

London Guildhall, site of London's Roman amphitheatre.

Plans were drawn up to construct a new gallery over the amphitheatre site, allowing public access to the lower level for viewing the archaeological remains, the ellipse of the arena partially marked out by an 80-metre-wide curved line of dark stone slabs on the Guildhall's paved yard. Toward the end of the second millennium, a team from the Museum of London uncovered the amphitheatre's south entrance, two public gateways, and a male skeleton laying below the entrance, believed to be a ritual burial of a gladiator.

First constructed around AD 70, and improved and enlarged during AD 120, measuring 105 metres by 85 metres, excavations revealed the open-air amphitheatre was originally constructed in timber, then later in stone, the walls plastered and brightly painted with additional decorative marble inlay work. From the high outer wall, banks of terracing provided seating for an estimated 7,000 spectators, which sloped down towards an inner wall encircling the arena.

Although no records exist of the type of activities taking place, to amuse and captivate the enthusiastic and bloodthirsty crowds attending Londinium's first theatre of entertainment, performances undoubtedly followed the traditions of other Roman amphitheatres. A venue for bloody executions, gladiatorial combats, and savage encounters between a variety of wild beasts, or between beast and man, entertainment included social comedies and dramas performed by a complement of actors, mostly trained slaves. London's Roman citizens would have attended both the gladiatorial exhibitions and staged dramatic performances, where both combatants and actors became legendary idols, much like today's sports and entertainment superstars.

The Romans brought with them their own cultural forms of entertainment, many derived from early Greek productions. Unlike the Greeks, however, whose theatrical preferences were melodrama and tragedy, Roman actors and their audiences favoured comedy along with dramatic storylines.

The early dramas and comedies written by Roman playwrights such as Terence, Plautus, and Caecilius involved legendary heroes, mistaken identities, lovers, and disguises, storylines which influenced the writings of future Renaissance playwrights.

Although it is very likely comedic drama was performed at London's Amphitheatre, by the time of its enlargement in the mid-third century, Roman plays had degenerated into acts known in Greek as *mimus*, bawdy farces performed by a troupe of players which for the first time included women, and *pantomimus,* a coarse dancing and singing act where a nonspeaking performer played all the characters accompanied by a group of singers, the chorus. These early *mimus* and *pantomimus* performances were the origins of today's mime and pantomime evolving in Britain during the eighteenth century, although they were much different productions from those played out at London's Amphitheatre.

By the early fourth century, a majority of Rome's military force had abandoned Britain, the city falling into disuse and decay, the amphitheatre laying dormant for several hundred years, and its stonework robbed to construct new buildings after the city was reoccupied during the eleventh century. By the twelfth century, all that remained of London's first performance space was buried below layers of rubble, before the Guildhall was erected upon the site.

2

London's Renaissance Theatre

After Roman occupation, no evidence has been found of any permanent performance places established inside or outside the old Roman walls up until early Tudor playhouses were established, a period when London's theatreland truly evolved.

Theatre survived mostly through wandering actors and minstrels performing in market squares and local fairs, occasionally erecting a temporary performance platform within halls, courtyards, or open spaces, anyplace where audiences were able to gather.

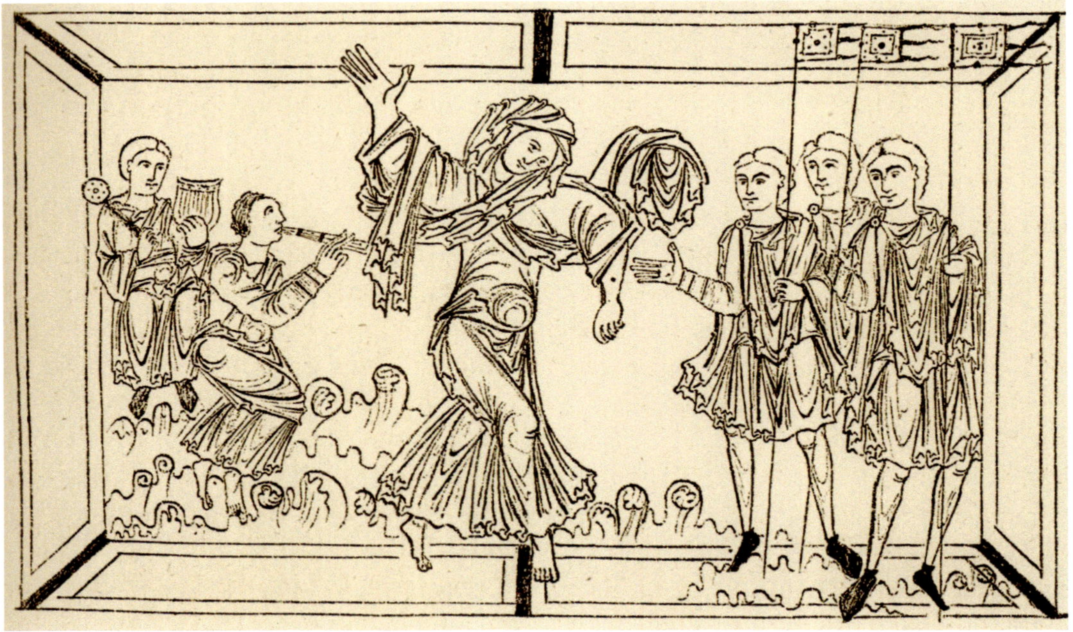

Musical interlude, eleventh century.

Many performances were based upon folktales and legends, stories retold and performed down through the centuries. Then, by the tenth century, the church encouraged dramatic performances known as Mystery Cycles constructed around biblical stories and major events in the Christian almanac, and Miracle plays, tales of the lives of saints, their endeavours and accomplishments, both types of performance used as a means for teaching Christian values to the illiterate.

It would be usual before each performance for a pageant of wagons to carry performers through the London streets, stopping at prearranged sites where the plays would then be acted out, and between the sixteenth to seventeenth centuries, many performances took place at Holy Priory Church on Leadenhall Street.

Miracle and Mystery plays came in for much criticism during the thirteenth century, with performances condemned for the blurring of divine and humanistic values. Following the Reformation, all religious dramas, which at the time were predominantly Catholic, were suppressed, and actors and acting companies were required to obtain a licence allowing them to rehearse and perform for the public, with a condition they secured the patronage from peers of prominence and a convert to the Church of England. From the

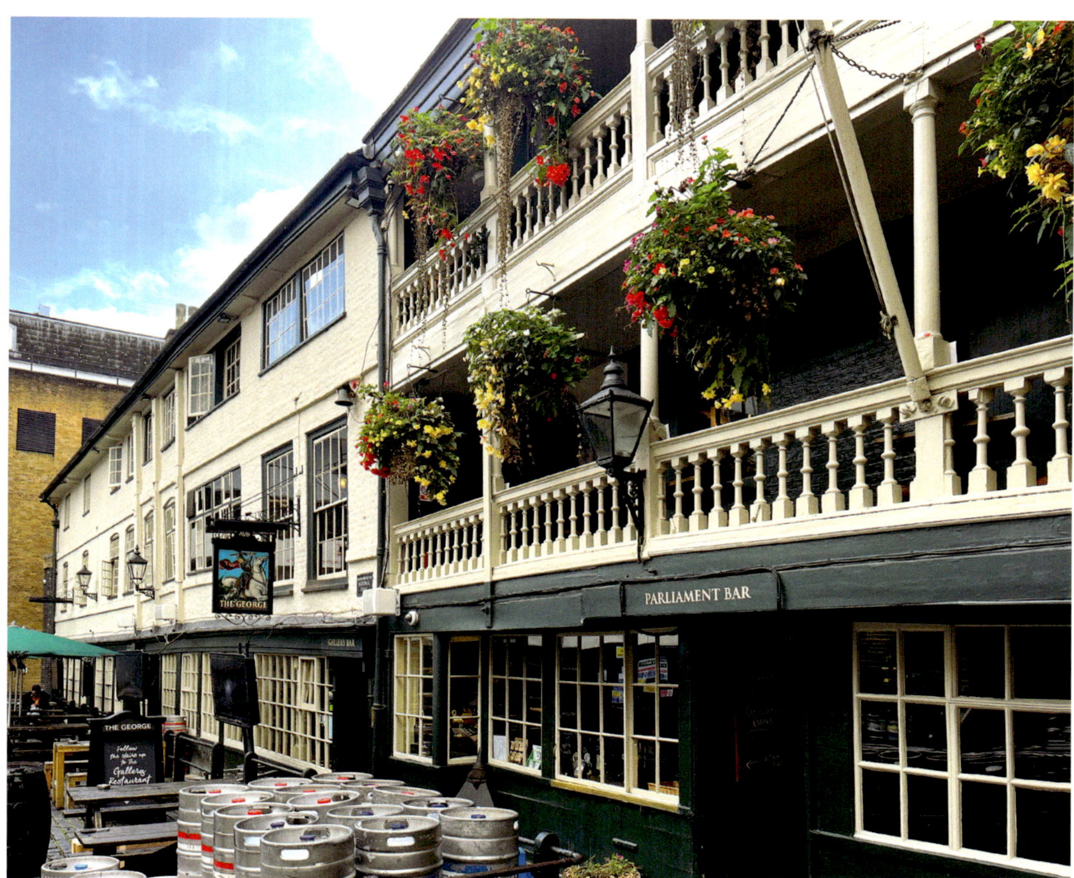

The George, Borough High Street.

mid-sixteenth century, hundreds of actors received licenses from noblemen to perform, the licensees then forming companies of players. Eventually, Miracle and Mystery plays became obsolete through the growth of professional theatre.

After the emergence of the English Renaissance in the early sixteenth century, a movement embracing literacy, music, and art, companies of travelling actors continued performing plays in open spaces and at fairs, guildhalls, halls of royalty and the nobility, and galleried courtyards of London inns. Referred to as inn-yard theatre, companies of actors performed at London inns such as the Boar's Head outside Aldgate, the Crosskeys in Gracechurch Street, the Bull Inn at Bishopsgate, and the White Hart Inn and George Inn at Southwark. The George Inn, off Borough High Street, now owned and leased by the National Trust, is the only London galleried inn to survive. Established during the Middle Ages and formally known as the George and Dragon, the inn was rebuilt in 1677, after a fire swept through Southwark destroying a majority of the timber-built properties.

Negotiating a performance fee with the innkeeper, a temporary stage would be erected in the courtyard and the public would be charged a fee to enter, paying extra to watch the play from the gallery. As plays became a popular form of entertainment for most classes of London's citizens, courtyard productions attracted some five to six hundred paying customers at each performance. In 1524, courtier John Rastell erected a private theatre at the rear of his property at Old Street, on the edge of the city boundary, and The Red Lion at Whitechapel had a permanent courtyard stage erected in 1567, possibly the first purposely built for public performances. At Newington Butts, south of the river toward the Elephant and Castle, Jerome Savage, a member of the Earl of Warwick's Company, converted an existing building into a performance venue known as the Playhouse, derived from the medieval word *pleghus*.

Through an increase in London's population and the popularity of plays, the City of London authorities began regulating courtyard performances. The actors, like many street entertainers from the period, were classed as beggars and vagabonds through an Act of Parliament in 1572. The London Mayor and the City of London then banned all plays as a measure against the spread of the plague through large audience gatherings, companies of actors forced to perform outside the city boundary, prompting the construction of playhouses beyond London's jurisdiction.

It is believed the first purpose-built playhouse, a polygon-shaped open-air building, was erected in 1576, at Finsbury Fields, just outside the city, known simply as The Theatre, the name taken from the Greek word, *theatrum* meaning 'a place for viewing'. The Theatre was built for members of the Earl of Leicester's household, known as Leicester's Men, formed in 1559, led by Bromley-born James Burbage. Another playhouse, the Curtain, was then established in an area of fields within the Curtain Estate close to The Theatre. The Curtain was possibly a converted existing lodging house, as excavation works provide evidence the building was rectangular rather than the recognised polygonal-shaped playhouse structure.

On the Southbank, known as a place for immoral activity and salubrious entertainment, with animal baiting and cockfighting, drinking, and prostitution, in 1587, impresario Philip Henslowe built The Rose, the first purpose-built playhouse in Southwark, the beginning of London's theatrical district south of the Thames.

The next built was The Swan in 1595, to the west of The Rose, and the most well-known playhouse of all, the Globe, erected in 1599 between both competitors, all three open to the air.

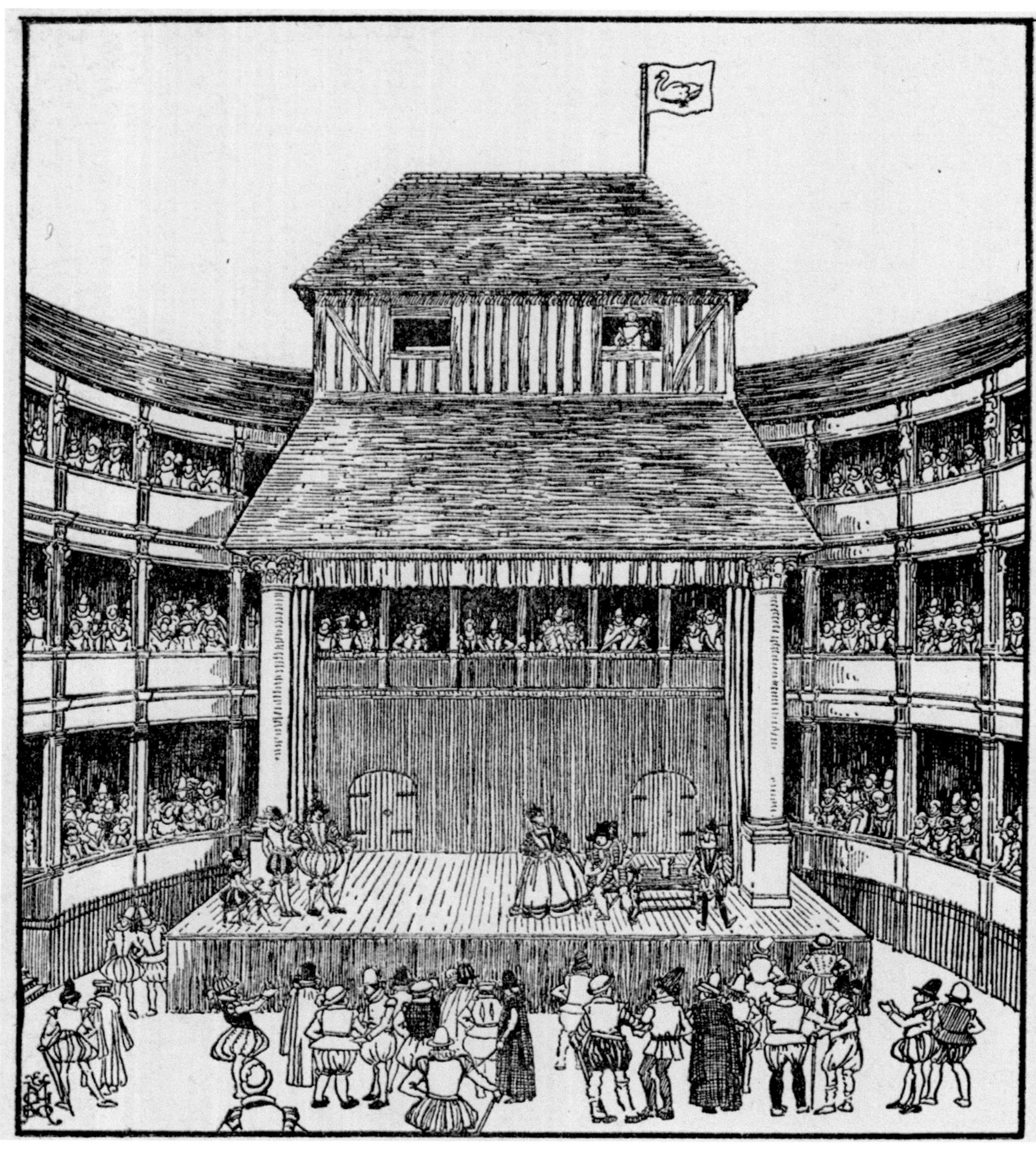

The Swan, Southwark, late sixteenth century.

The Globe playhouse was built using robbed material from The Theatre, which Burbage had taken down and transported across the river after a dispute with landlord Giles Allen, claiming he took possession of the playhouse from Burbage's father, who built The Theatre, after the lease expired.

The first performance at the Globe was reputedly Shakespeare's *Julius Caesar*, which took place in the spring of 1599. Able to house an audience or around 3,000, the cheapest entry fee was one penny to stand among the groundlings in the pit, a yard area surrounding the protruding stage.

A further penny secured a bench seat in the covered galleries, built in the fashion of the galleried inns. The pit was open to the elements, and performances took place during daylight, not only due to difficulties in lighting the stage but also because of the dangers playhouse-goers faced walking the streets at night.

After entering the Globe, money to attend the performance was placed in the slot of a sealed box, to prevent pilfering, and when full would be taken to a side office then broken open and the money counted, the origins of theatre box offices. The stage, built of timber projecting out into the pit, was partially covered towards the rear by a thatched roof, erected above a gallery mostly used to accommodate musicians, although the gallery balcony would often be used by actors during a performance, such as the balcony scene in Shakespeare's *Romeo and Juliet*. The roof was supported by pillars with a space between them to allow people on each side of the playhouse a see the actors performing. Below the stage gallery, a large space came into use throughout performances, with entry and exit points for actors. The stage scenery was minimalistic, as spoken words, the actors' performances, dramatic action scenes, and special effects were the most important aspects of conveying the essence of a play.

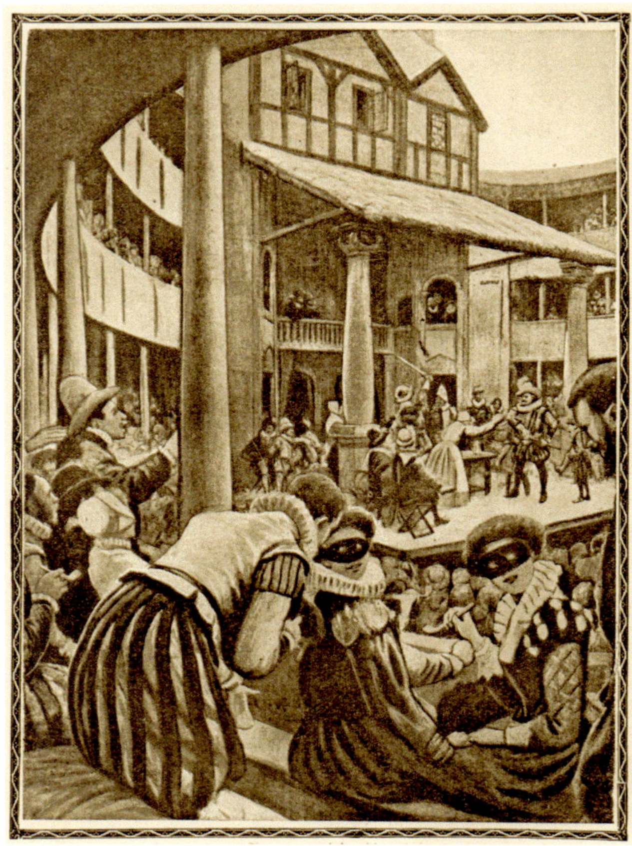

Globe Theatre, Southwark, 1599.

Special effects had first been used in miracle plays, especially when depicting crucifixions and executions, animal blood, and intestines used to imitate the real thing. During the sixteenth century, spectacular special effects would increase audience numbers, and profits for the playhouse. Ghosts and spirits suddenly rose up from a trap door through a cloud of smoke or swept down from above as if in flight, an actor suspended on a swinging rope. Actors meticulously rehearsed scenes of combat, popular in history plays performed during the 1500s and 1600s, using prop swords, pistols, muskets, and cannons, effects which did not always go to plan. In 1613, during a performance of *Henry VIII*, a misfire of a prop cannon resulted in the Globe's thatch roof catching alight and the playhouse burning down.

Rebuilt within a year, with the addition of a tiled roof, the Globe is associated with whom many consider the greatest playwright in British history, William Shakespeare, a member of the Lord Chamberlain's company and playhouse shareholder.

There has been much speculation concerning the man from Stratford-upon-Avon as to whether Shakespeare was the author of all the plays and sonnets attributed to him. Contemporaries of Shakespeare also wrote plays for the Globe, such as John Fletcher, Ben Johnson, and Thomas Middleton, and it is believed that, from surviving evidence,

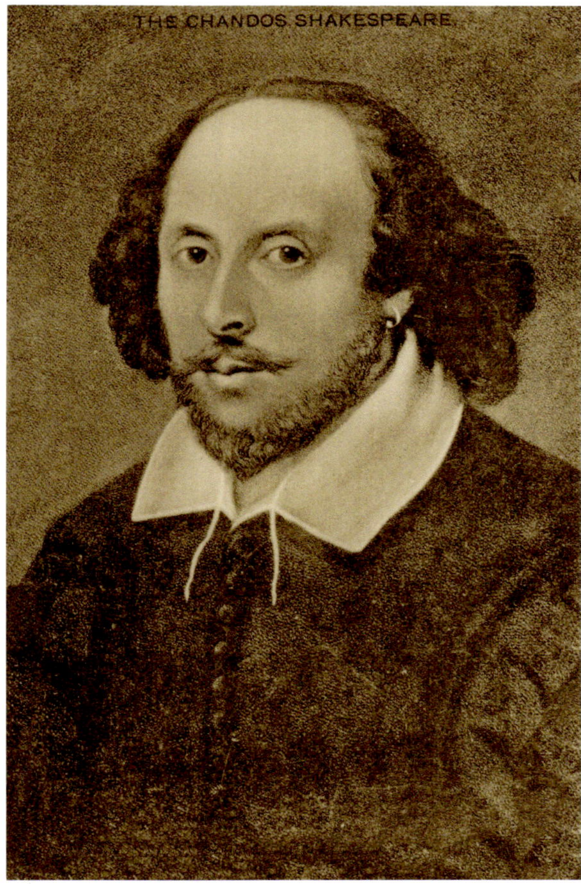

Portrait of Shakespeare, owned by the 3rd Duke of Chandos, mid-1700s, believed to be the most accurate depiction.

Shakespeare collaborated with other playwrights, along with adapting and rewriting existing plays from earlier times. There is no doubt, however, that during Shakespeare's theatrical career, the character of drama, written and performed, transformed theatre in London, the playhouses flourishing through the variety of plays produced – histories, comedies, and tragedies.

Before the Globe caught fire, Rose owner Philip Henslowe, whose diary was a primary source of information for Renaissance London theatre, engaged the carpenter who constructed the Globe to erect a playhouse, the Fortune, at Cripplegate, to maximise his income by attracting a higher class of clientele from the merchants, trades, and guilds of the city, as well as members of the inns of court, people who rarely ventured south of the Thames. Shakespeare's company also travelled north of the river to perform at Blackfriars, the playhouse evolving from the former Blackfriars Friary located within the western city boundary.

It was around this period when many playhouses became enclosed and lit with candles, the plays performed to smaller, private audiences, a higher entrance fee prohibiting attendance by the lower, poorer, classes. Food and drink were available to purchase during intervals, a break in the play established as a means to replace burned-down candles, and additional music and songs were introduced as the enclosed venue offered superior acoustics. One aspect of theatre that did not change, however, was acting companies were made up entirely of men.

Although the acting profession was looked upon poorly by both the church and city authority, allowing women to appear on stage was considered a threat to the male hierarchy, and acting companies performed on stage with the exclusion of women, all

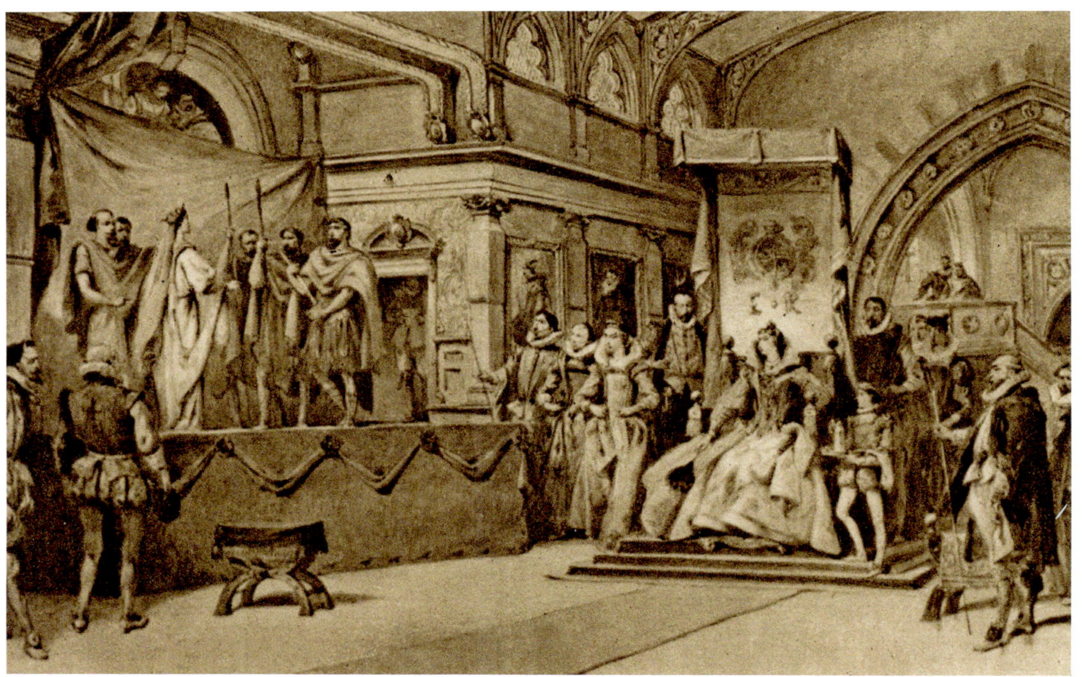

Shakespeare performing at the royal court of Elizabeth I, late 1500s.

female roles being played by youthful feminine-looking actors. Nevertheless, women were not absent from the theatre world; a few were involved in the business side of the profession on behalf of their playhouse owner husbands, and later women were engaged in costume making, when actors' costumes became a significant visual aspect of a play. Generally, most actors wore day-to-day clothing, or the company's donated clothes. Then, as new, bright, and colourful costumes were required, an industry of theatrical costumers and wigmakers evolved around London's theatre districts, many run and staffed by women.

A few women would later take to the stage of playhouses, inns, and tobacco shops, entertaining audiences by playing musical instruments and singing songs. One such entertainer was Mary Frith, also known as Moll Cutpurse, a self-proclaimed cross-dresser, underworld fence, thief, and solicitor of male and female prostitutes. After making her name through acts of criminality and a flamboyant lifestyle, Frith featured in a production written about her by Thomas Middleton and Thomas Decker, *The Roaring Girl*, performed at the Fortune Playhouse, Finsbury. The role of Frith was played by a male actor; however, it was said that Frith often appeared at the side of the stage dressed as a man, playing upon a lute while singing lude songs.

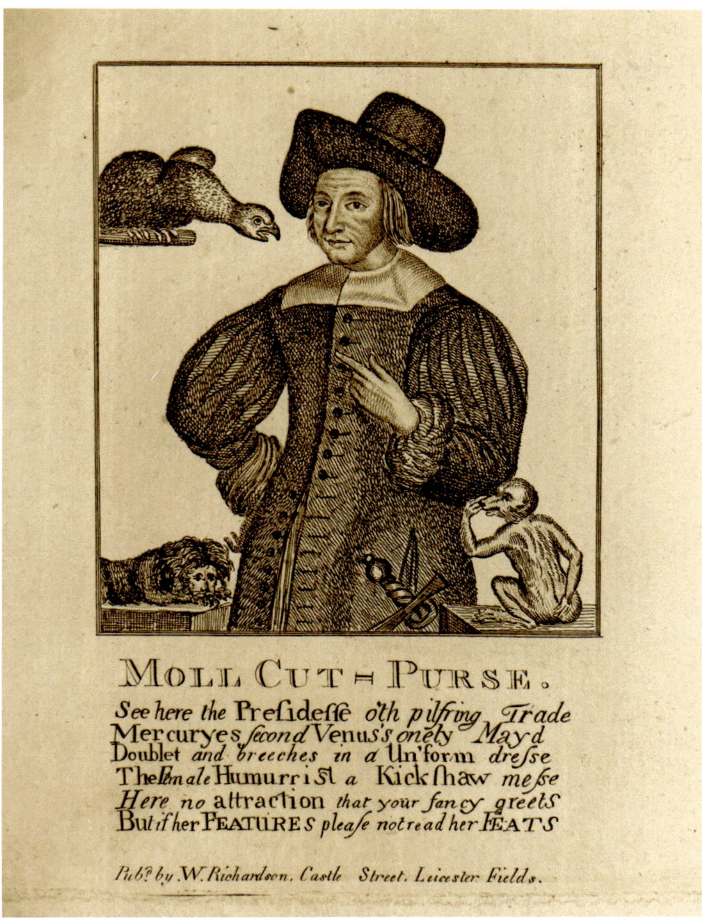

Moll Cutpurse
(Mary Frith), early 1600s.
(Wellcome Collection)

When a troupe of French players performed at Blackfriars in 1629, under the patronage of Queen Henrietta Maria, unusually women performed alongside men, and it has been suggested that while the future King of England, Charles II, was in exile he witnessed actresses performing in French plays, influencing Charles to permit women to act on stage after the Restoration.

South of the river at Bankside, the playhouses and galleried inns were flourishing. Nonetheless, its reputation as a place of depravity and immorality remained a concern to London's disapproving authorities.

Theatregoing had become a favourite leisure pursuit for a majority of London's society, and by the time James I came to the throne in 1603, many playwrights were producing new material for London's twenty or more playhouses, located north and south of the Thames, and at London's four Inns of Court, colleges for educating young men to enter the legal profession, where gala performances of plays and masques were performed.

Customarily staged on festive occasions in the homes of the nobility, masques, a form of entertainment that originated in Italy, were played out in imaginary settings with elaborate scenery and fantastic costumes, the scenery and costumes often designed by eminent architects of the time. The company of amateur actors, frequently courtiers who included women, hid their faces behind decorated masks during performances of drama, dance, music, and poetry.

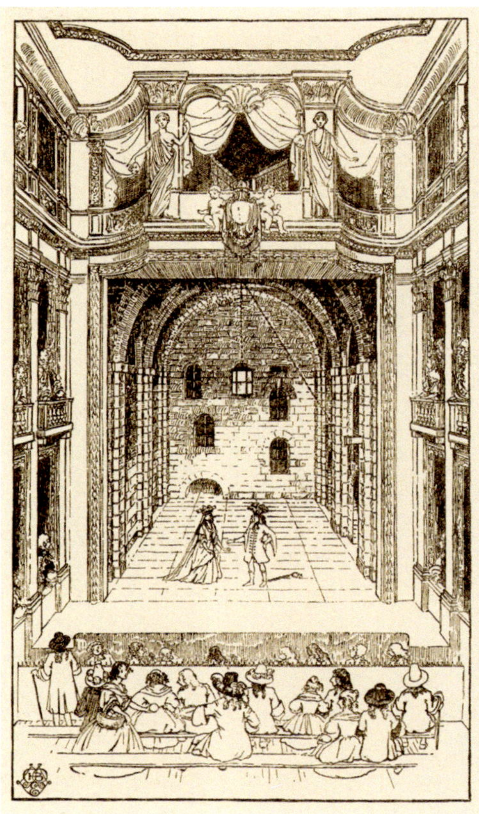

Enclosed mid-seventeenth-century playhouse.

Unlike public plays, the audience consisted of a small number of invited guests, who would then join in towards the performance finale. Over time, masques developed into their own form of entertainment and were performed in many of London's public theatres.

Despite much-continued condemnation by London authority, theatre had become a flourishing business, and several more playhouses had been built outside, and inside, the city boundary. The Boars Head Inn at Aldgate was converted into a playhouse in 1598, along with the Red Bull Inn at St John Street in 1607, and within the city, a successor to Blackfriars was established in 1609. St Paul's Cathedral had its own playhouse within its precinct, and Philip Henslowe opened the Porters Hall in 1615. Further playhouses were also established to the west: Whitefriars Playhouse in 1608, the Phoenix in 1616, a converted cockpit and the first theatre built close to Drury Lane, and Salisbury Court Playhouse in 1629.

London's most exclusive theatre, Whitehall Playhouse Theatre, designed by Indigo Jones, was the furthest west, and although open to the public, audiences were mostly members of London's elite society. Under the patronage of Queen Elizabeth I, the cast at the Whitehall Playhouse Theatre were generally companies of younger actors, such as The Paul's Boys, choristers from St Paul's Cathedral, which offered them an opportunity to show off their talents performing to royalty and courtiers in the most sumptuous surroundings.

During the reign of James I, keen young playwrights, alongside old stagers such as Shakespeare and Ben Johnson, began writing plays that would embrace violent plotlines of revenge and moral corruption, some even including scenes of incest, rape, and mutilation, which although popular with the public, gave the rising Puritan movement, hostile to theatrical entertainment, more reason to campaign for the closure of London playhouses.

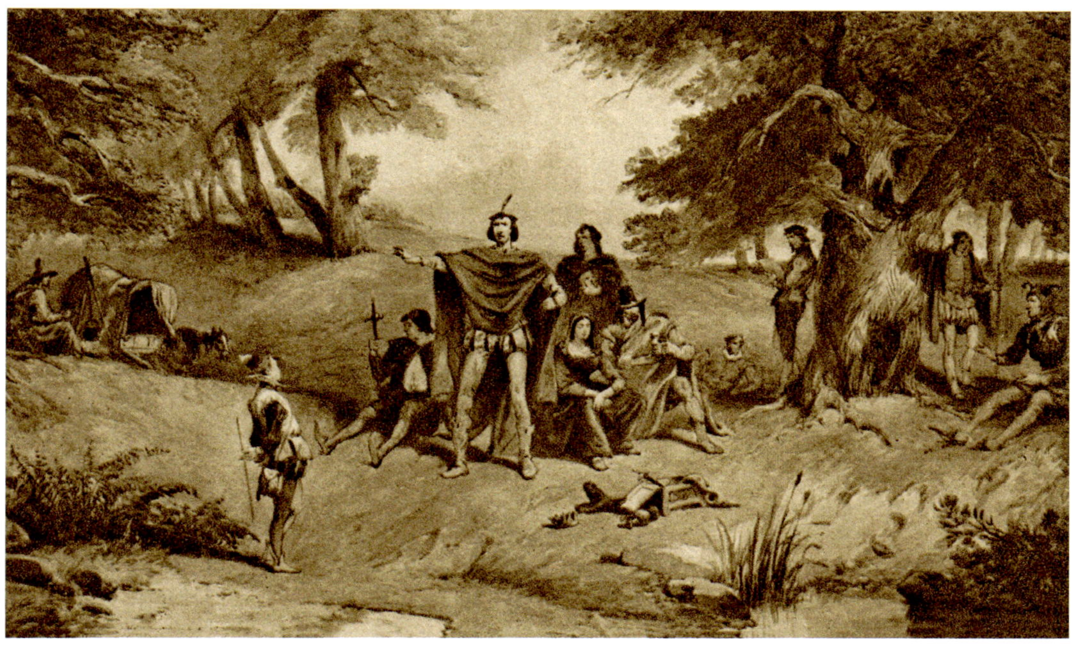

Shakespeare's strolling players rehearsing in the countryside, late 1500s.

Despite all this, the first forced closures came through bouts of plague, common throughout London, and the fear playhouse gatherings would spread the disease amongst the city's population, which left acting companies no alternative but to escape London and tour the provinces to earn a living.

James I was an enthusiastic devotee of theatre and commissioned several plays to be written and performed in private at Whitehall Palace, where the great hall, great chamber, and Elizabethan-built canvas and timber banqueting house were regularly in use as performance spaces. As the old banqueting house was not up to the standard required by the king, it was rebuilt to a design by architect Robert Stickells and completed in 1608, specifically to hold royal receptions, theatrical performances, and masque balls. The building, however, was destroyed by fire ten years later and replaced by Inigo Jones's elegant Palladian-style structure, surviving a fire that burned down Whitehall Palace in 1698.

By the end of the same century, many of London's Elizabethan- and Jacobean-built playhouses had also gone, after the closure of London's theatres in 1642, to prevent public disorder when Oliver Cromwell and the Puritans gained power after King Charles I was defeated in the English Civil War. Although the ban lasted for eighteen years, theatre closures brought about the emergence of musical performances popular in Europe: the opera. It is believed that Cromwell discovered a means to appease a population missing their theatrical entertainment, a period when musical performances were allowed and plays were not, by permitting opera, after reading a pamphlet written by Charles I's poet laureate William Davenant, rumoured to be Shakespeare's illegitimate son. The pamphlet extolled the virtues of opera, compared to the pre-Civil War lewd and socially offensive plays, suggesting opera could well become a righteous form of entertainment promoting Puritan ideals. Although a supporter of the Royalists and having spent some time imprisoned in the Tower of London, Davenant was pardoned and later staged an operatic performance, *The Siege of Rhodes*, in 1656 before a paying audience at a private theatre, Rutland House, Aldersgate. Believed to have been the first performance of an English opera, the cast included the first known unofficial female actress-singer, Catherine Coleman, wife of composer and countertenor Edward Coleman.

So popular was this first opera, in reality, an underhand means to have plays performed to the public but accompanied by music, Davenant wrote a sequel, and then two dramas in support of Cromwell's foreign policy, undoubtedly to ensure support of the Protectorate.

After the death of Cromwell and the crowning of Charles II, English opera evolved gradually throughout the late seventeenth century and into the eighteenth century when the first ever season of opera was performed at the Theatre Royal, Covent Garden. On the return of the monarchy, theatres that reopened were prohibited from performing serious spoken drama, unless awarded a Letter of Patent, a licence issued by Charles II. Letters of Patent were awarded to Davenant who founded The Dukes Company and converted a tennis court into a theatre at Lincoln's Inn Fields, and dramatist and royal master of the revels Thomas Killigrew, establishing the King's Company.

The upsurge of theatrical development west of the city began when Killigrew built the Theatre Royal Drury Lane, the oldest London theatre site still in use, managed by actor and grandnephew of Shakespeare, Charles Hart. With a capacity of 700, the Theatre Royal was a three-tier wooden building, with an open roof above the pit surrounded by semicircular covered galleries on three levels. Although surviving the Great Fire of London, the Theatre Royal caught fire and burned down in 1672.

Letters of Patent were then reissued to both companies with a revision permitting women to perform on stage professionally with the provision that all female parts should be played by women unless there was a shortage of actresses, in which case young men could continue playing female roles.

Following the years of zealous Puritan authoritarianism, allowing women the opportunity to appear professionally on stage resulted in a radical change in the theatrical establishment, and an increase in men attending performances to witness attractive women on stage, who, in many Restoration productions, often appeared in a state of semi-undress, and unsurprisingly, the introduction of females acting on stage became an enormous success.

The first accredited appearance of an actress in a dramatic role on stage was Margaret Hughes, the mistress of Prince Rupert of the Rhine, playing the part of Desdemona in a production of *Othello* at the King's Company's Vere Street Theatre, the converted tennis court near Lincoln's Inn Fields, in December 1660. A month later, theatregoer and social diarist Samuel Pepys wrote of the first time he witnessed a woman appearing on stage, in the comedy *Beggar's Bush*.

The first theatrical performance Charles II attended after the Restoration was at The Duke of York's Theatre, situated on the riverfront at Dorset Street, a small venue believed

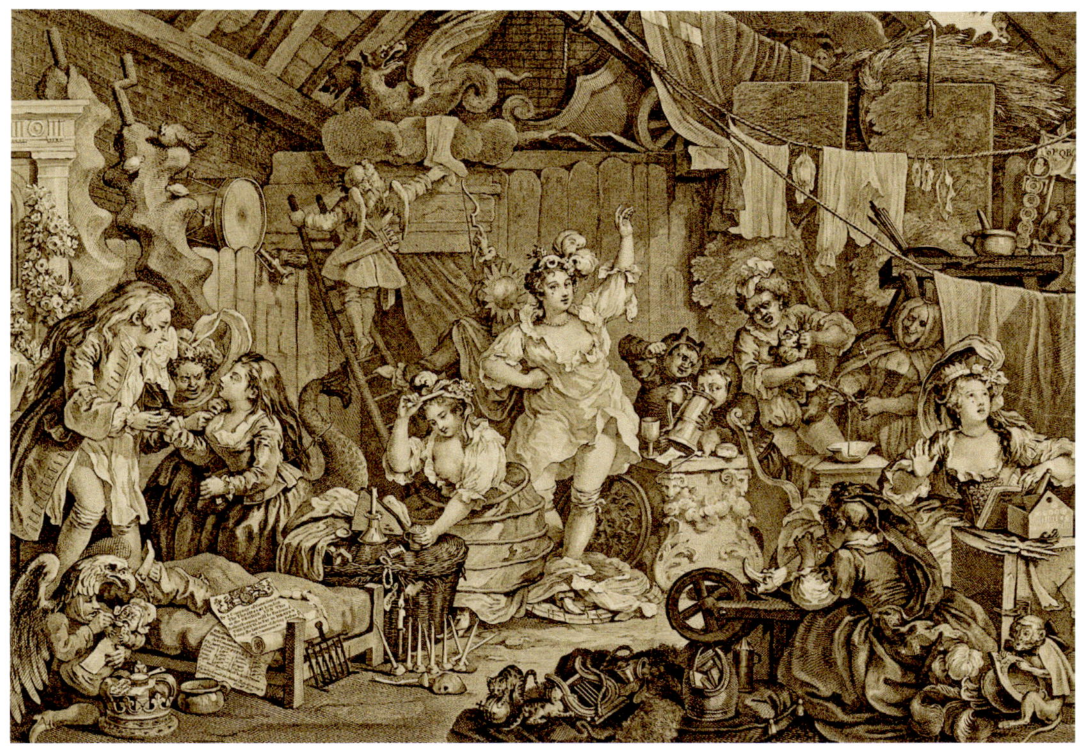

Strolling actresses dressing in a barn, early 1700s. Engraving by W. Hogarth. (Wellcome Collection)

to have been designed by Sir Christopher Wren, when theatre performances at the time mostly consisted of revivals of various Shakespeare plays and adaptations of plays suiting modern times, with very few new plays written for the stage. The comedies and tragedies that followed, known as Reformation plays, often rebelled against the former Puritan regime, with purposely designed ostentatious and colourful costumes for the leading players, women and men, along with extravagant and elaborately created scenery.

Just three years after the reopening of London's theatreland a bout of plague spread through London forcing the playhouses to close again. When it seemed this devastating malady had done its worst, after a lengthy period of drought, a small fire that broke out on Pudding Lane in September 1666 soon grew into an inferno that raged for five days, engulfing much of the old City of London.

While most of London's purpose-built theatres were outside of the city wall, a majority of the buildings, halls, and inns within the city, utilised as playhouses, fell victim to the fire, along with the Salisbury Court playhouse, to the west of the city wall. Although both the plague and fire could well have had a diverse effect on the wealth and spending power of London, the destruction of its dilapidated medieval buildings and squalid residential housing offered an opportunity to rebuild the city. Under instruction from Charles II, architects such as Christopher Wren, Valentine Knight, John Vanbrugh, and Robert Hook envisaged a new baroque-style London, and with the city's rebirth, to the west, Drury Lane, Covent Garden and Strand would evolve and emerge as London's theatrical capital.

A patron of the arts and enthusiastic theatregoer, Charles II's theatrical passions extended to an off-stage liaison with celebrity figure and Restoration actress, former orange seller eighteen-year-old Nell Gwyn, who the king took as his mistress. Before her relationship with the king, Gwyn, besides selling oranges, sold gin as a child to clients at a brothel in Macklin Street, close to the Theatre Royal, and at the age of fifteen became the lover of Charles Hart. Gwyn was one of the first recognised female stage performers alongside contemporaries including Elizabeth Barry, famed for performing tragedy; Anne Bracegirdle, excelling when playing heroines; and Mary Saunderson, recognised as the first female to portray Juliet, in Shakespeare's *Romeo and Juliet*.

It was said at the time that Gwyn, as an actress, was acknowledged more for her looks than her talent; however, diarist and social critic Samuel Pepys raved over Gwyn's performance and comic abilities when playing Florimell in *The Maiden Queen*, a comic tragedy by John Dryden, performed by the King's Company at Drury Lane in 1667. Shortly after taking up with the king, Gwyn retired from the stage, giving birth to Charles II's seventh son in 1670.

Five years after Gwyn appeared in *The Maiden Queen* the play was performed by an all-female cast. It was not, however, the first time women had been cast in every role, as King's Company manager, Thomas Killigrew, staged his own bawdy comedy embracing sexual freedom: *The Parson's Wedding* in 1664, a sensation at that time. During the summer of 1667, there came a series of all-female plays performed by the King's Company, which, alongside *The Parson's Wedding* and *The Maiden Queen*, included a revival of a Jacobean tragic-comedy *Philastar*, by Francis Beaumont and John Fletcher.

London's theatreland was comparatively small in comparison to the modern-day West End, and several of the old playhouses and theatres closed after the Civil War, which were no longer fit for purpose. The few playhouses that survived, however, were refurbished

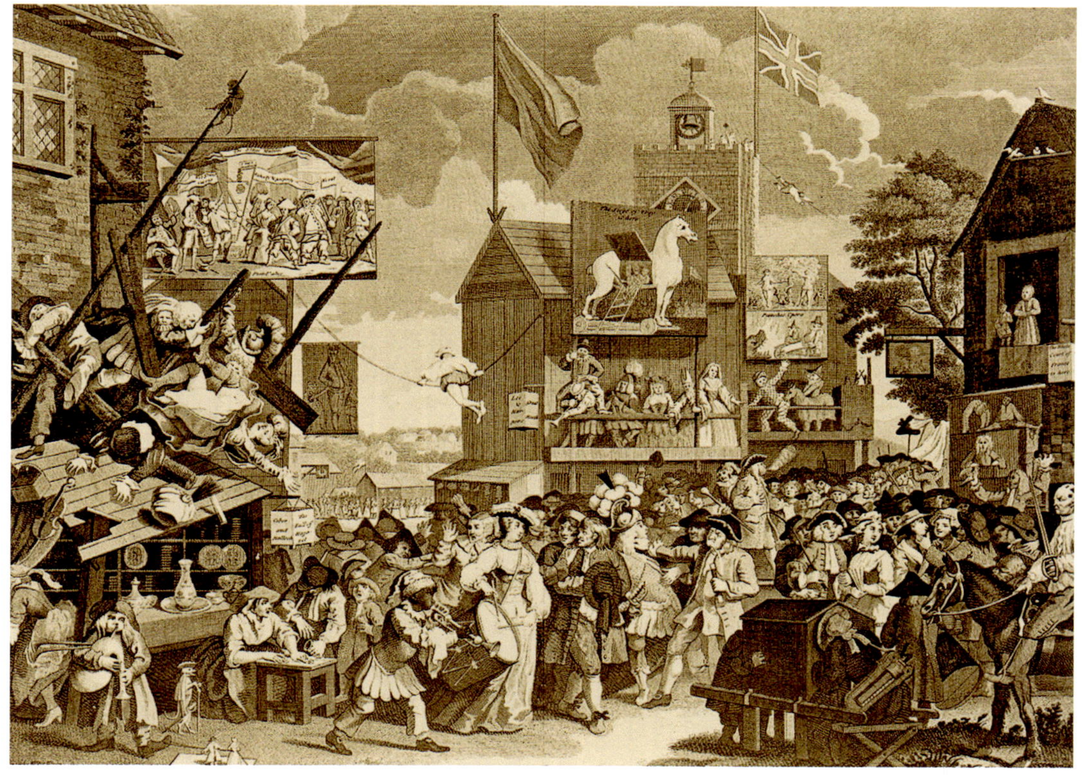

Southwark Fair, renowned place of amusement, late 1700s. Engraving by T. Cook after W. Hogarth. (Wellcome Collection)

or rebuilt. South of the Thames, when Bankside began a period of transformation, from a place of immorality and raucous entertainment to an area of emerging industry, playhouses such as the Globe, Rose, and Swan had also disappeared, demolished to make way for warehouses alongside tenements erected for workers and their families.

All evidence of the existence of Bankside's Tudor and Jacobean theatres was lost up until the late 1900s when the remains of two playhouses were discovered during construction work excavations. The foundations of the Rose theatre were unearthed during an archaeological dig before planned large-scale redevelopment of a site on Park Street, adjacent to Southwark Bridge, important remains that could well have been destroyed by construction workers unaware of the site's significance and eager to move forward with the office development.

A 'Save The Rose' campaign started by prominent theatrical artists, including Sir Laurance Olivier, Dame Peggy Ashcroft, and American Sam Wanamaker, who was in the process of attempting to recreate the Globe, halted the work and volunteers stood guard over the site until the playhouse received protected status. The new proposed office block was redesigned to bridge the remains of the Rose, protected in a space below, its foundations marked out in red lights and covered by a shallow layer of water preventing decay of the archaeological site. The enclosed space below the office block was opened to the public

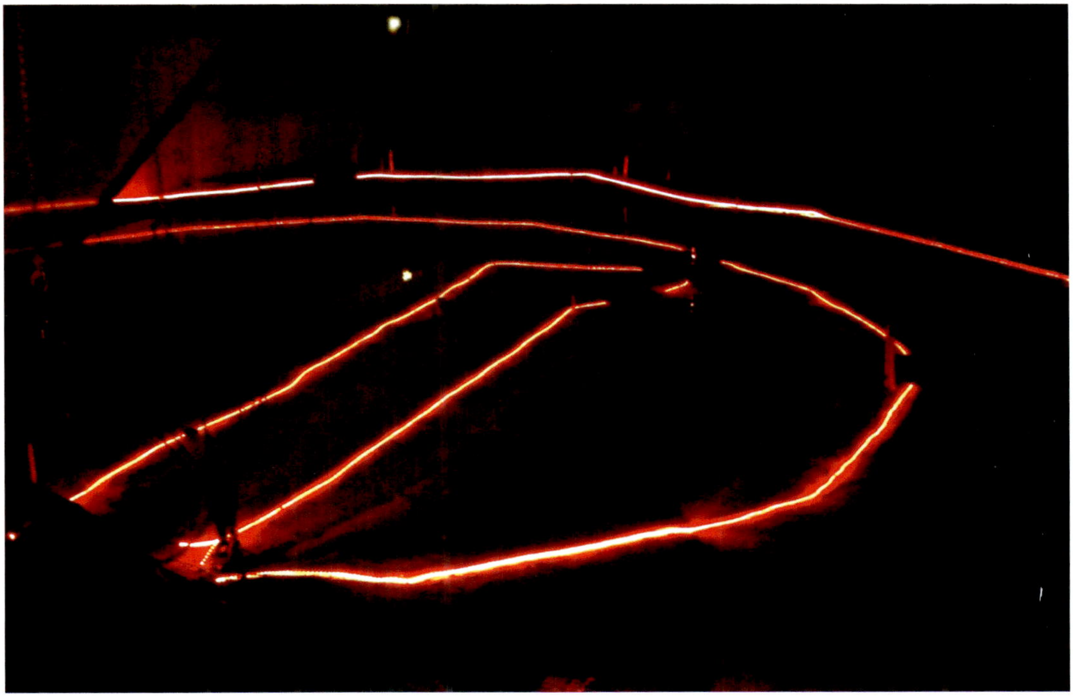

Protected remains of the Rose, 2012.

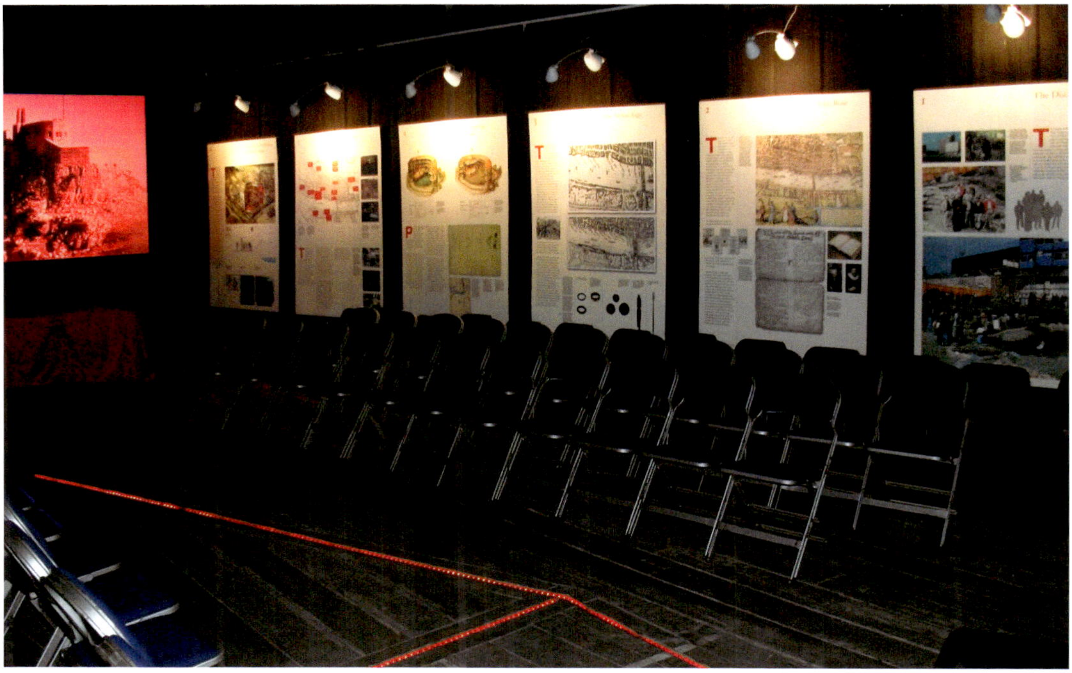

Rose contemporary performance space, 2012.

in 1999, and three years later regular performances of Shakespeare's plays were staged in the small undercroft adjacent to the playhouse remains.

Later in the same year, almost opposite the Rose, remains of the Globe were unearthed during site excavations of a former brewery car park, the foundations of the first playhouse, which burned down, along with remains of the second. The remnants consisted of the base of three walls, bricks and chalk blocks, and a layer of crushed hazelnut shells. It was popular at the time for theatregoers to eat snacks during performances usually consisting of hazelnuts, the shells discarded and dropped on the ground, then left in situ, the crushed casings used as ground covering.

The remains of the Globe were preserved and covered over to protect the site, however, much of the playhouse, which lies below a row of historic nineteenth-century houses, has yet to be excavated.

Both sites have provided substantial indication of the size, layout, and structure of early playhouses, instrumental in the design and construction of the recreated Globe on Bankside, which opened to the public in 1997, and the Rose at Kingston, opening in early 2008.

Returning to the nineteenth century, it was a period when bawdy, highly sexualised Restoration performances came under increasing public censure as London's middle-class theatregoers began flocking to these performances, theatre critic Jeremy Collier specifically damning architect and playwright Sir John Vanbrugh's controversial *Virtue of Danger* and *The Provok'd Wife* for their licentious plotlines.

At the time, the two major theatrical companies were also in conflict over securing the very best actors. Vanbrugh wrote *Virtue of Danger,* also known as *The Relapse,* specifically for the company at Drury Lane. The company, however, was on the brink of folding up as many actors had been bribed to defect to the company at Covent Garden.

The first performance of *Virtue of Danger* was a huge success and the takings from the run saved the company from bankruptcy. Turning his hand to architecture, after designing Castle Howard in Yorkshire, Vanbrugh was appointed controller of the Queen's works and in 1703 secured a commission to design the Queen's Theatre on the Haymarket.

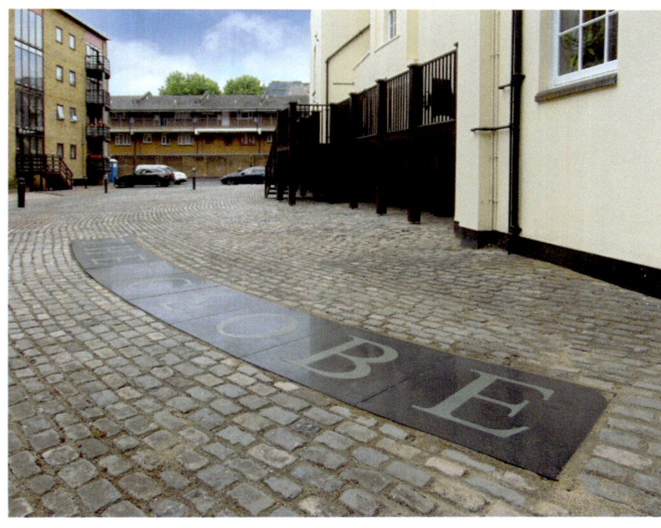

Remains of the Globe below courtyard paving and listed properties. The outer wall is marked by paving slabs.

3

Curtain Rises on Eighteenth-century Theatre

From the early 1700s, many new theatres were not only established in London, but also in towns and cities across the country, and much like in Shakespeare's time, strolling players took plays into the provinces, although largely to middle-class audiences.

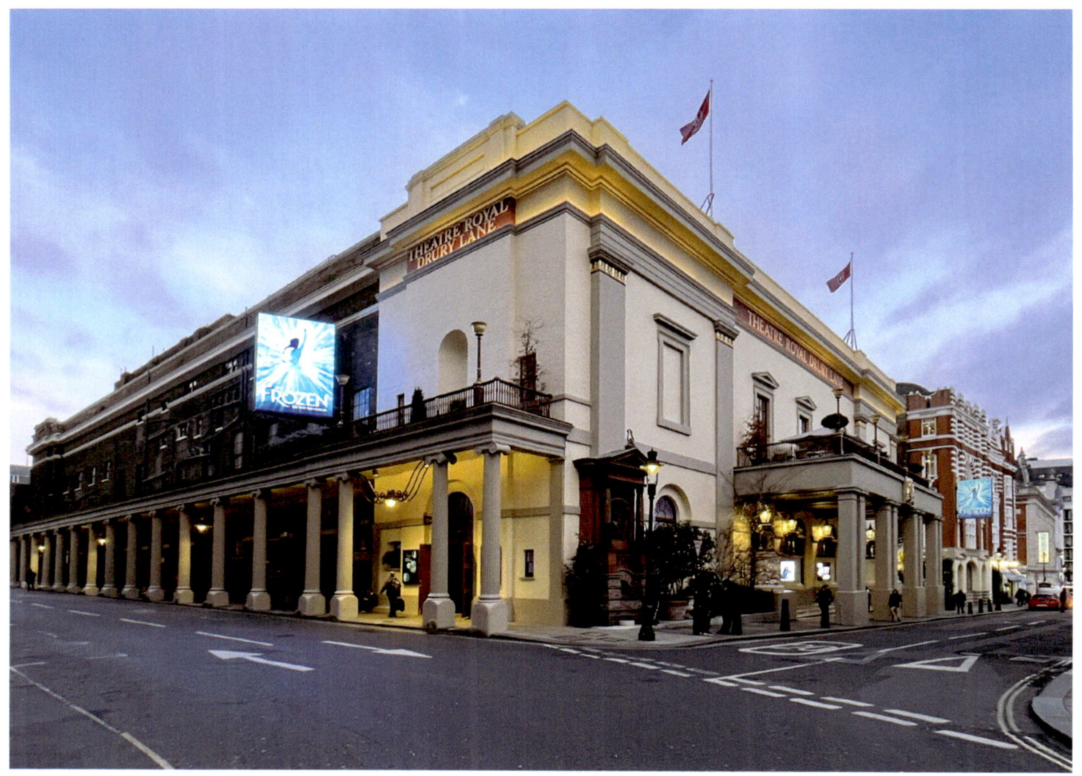

Known as the Theatre Royal Drury Lane, the main entrance is actually on Catherine Street.

Up until the late 1700s, many new London theatres were relatively small in size; however, the Theatre Royal, built by actor and theatrical impresario John Rich at Covent Garden, which opened in 1732, was larger than most. Both Theatre Royals, Drury Lane and the newly built theatre at Covent Garden, were the only two in London at the time permitted to perform spoken drama, then just two years after built, Covent Garden staged its first ballet, and a year later the theatre held a season of Handel's operas. Rich, who made a fortune promoting *The Beggar's Opera*, which premiered at Lincoln's Inn Fields in 1728, before performed at Covent Garden, was also notable for popularising pantomimes, appearing as Harlequin in each production finale.

A third theatre named Theatre Royal, built on the site of the Kings Head Inn, Haymarket, in 1720, also the third public theatre to open in the West End, was granted a royal patent in 1766 to perform legitimate plays, although only during the summer months. For the rest of the year performances comprised of opera and comedy musical entertainment.

On many occasions, comedy performances parodied and made light of the government and its ministerial members. The consequence of this led to free speech in the theatre

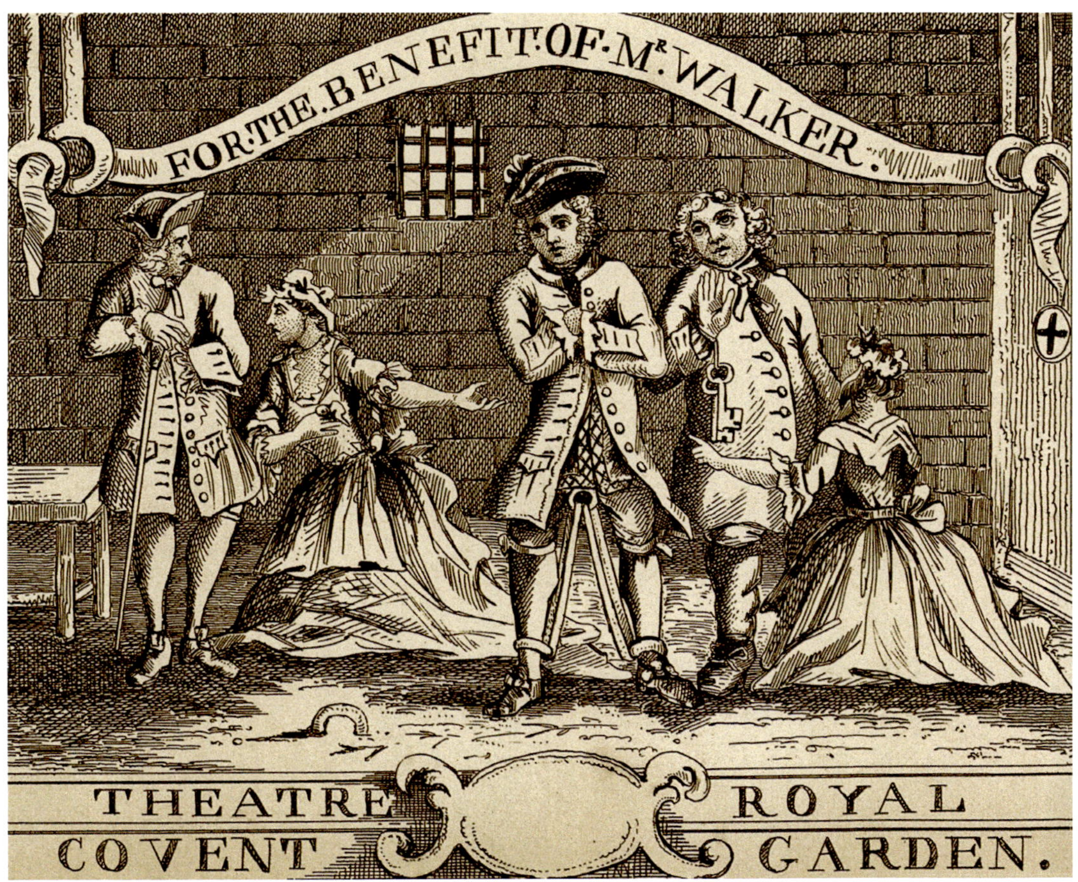

Scene from *The Beggar's Opera*: the Highwayman Macheath in prison. Etching after W. Hogarth. (Wellcome Collection)

becoming considered a threat and possible cause of social unrest and insurrection, resulting in the introduction of the Licensing Act 1737, an attempt to censor theatrical productions. After the Act was passed, which, with revisions, lasted until 1968, all plays were submitted to an examiner before issued a license. It is believed a satire aimed to lampoon George II and Prime Minister Sir Robert Walpole, *The Golden Rump*, written anonymously, was the deciding factor in the Act coming into force.

Although the play's authorship has been debated, dramatist Henry Fielding, who wrote under the pen name Captain Hercules Vinegar, H. Scriblerus Secundus, as well as producing work anonymously, is believed to have written the play. Author of *Tom Jones*, a series of best-selling publications encompassing the title character's life of love and virtue, Fielding was also a magistrate, appointed justice of the peace in 1748, allotted a courthouse and residence on Bow Street, adjacent to the theatre at Covent Garden.

From here, Fielding and his blind half-brother John, also a magistrate, presided over cases brought before them, suppressing crime by recruiting a band of able-bodied men known as 'theiftakers', referred to as Bow Street Runners. By the mid-eighteenth century, the Covent Garden piazza had become a salacious place of entertainment, where theatre audiences, a mixture of both upper and lower classes, came along in their hundreds nightly. Many, however, were often bad-mannered and extremely discourteous.

It was also well known that after attending the theatre, men of a certain fervour slipped away down a side street to engage one of many Covent Garden prostitutes, known as 'spells' or 'flash mollishers', while other men, whose preferences were male prostitutes, made their way to a local 'Molly House', John Fielding at the time referring to Covent Garden as the 'Great Square of Venus'.

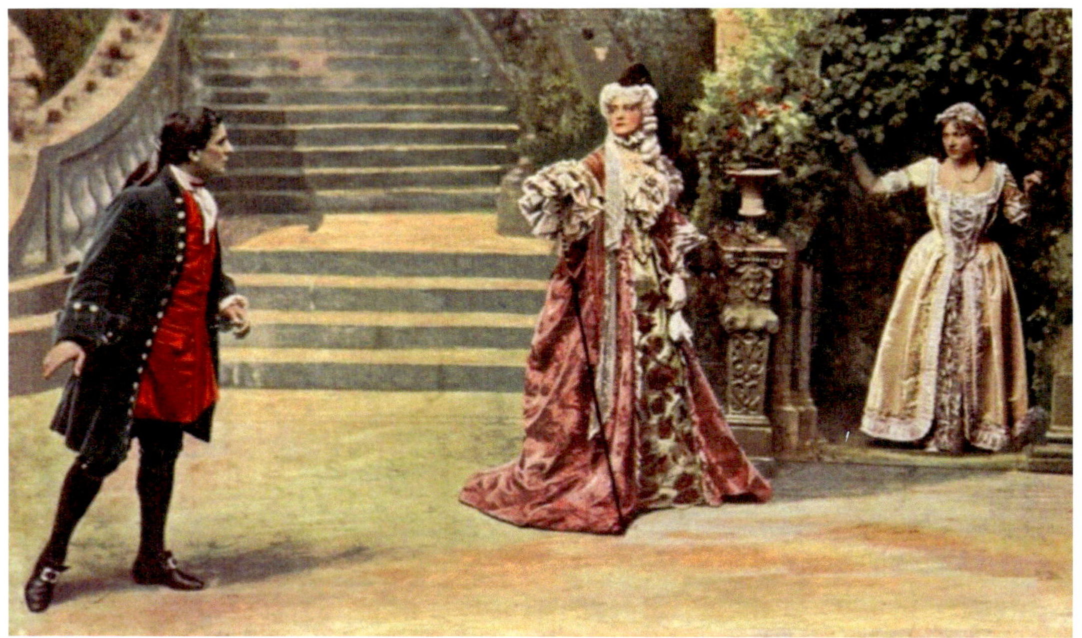

Operatic adaptation of Henry Fielding's *Tom Jones*, the Apollo, 1907.

Although there were very few exceptional theatre playwrights during the Georgian period, many great actors were treading the boards, most turning professional after performing in amateur productions. One such actor, David Garrick, who began a career as a wine trader before turning to acting, made his London debut as Richard III, at Goodman's Fields Theatre, Whitechapel, in 1741.

Earning rave reviews, Garrick was engaged to perform plays at Drury Lane, securing a place with the company for five years. His earnings as an actor enabled him to purchase shares in the theatre.

Considered the greatest actor of his age, Garrick appeared alongside many other leading actors and actresses, emerging to become the most important figure in London's theatreland, as a performer, manager, producer, and writer. In 1776, playwright Richard Sheridan bought Garrick's shares in Drury Lane, opening with his own play, *The Rivals*.

Even though Sheridan was a celebrated playwright, he was poor at organisation and began holding rehearsals before finishing the script. Garrick returned to take charge of theatrical proceedings while Sheridan completed one of his most well-known Georgian comedies, *The School for Scandal*, which was followed by another hit, *The Critic*. Through his success, Sheridan was able to rebuild and enlarge Drury Lane in 1794, which had a

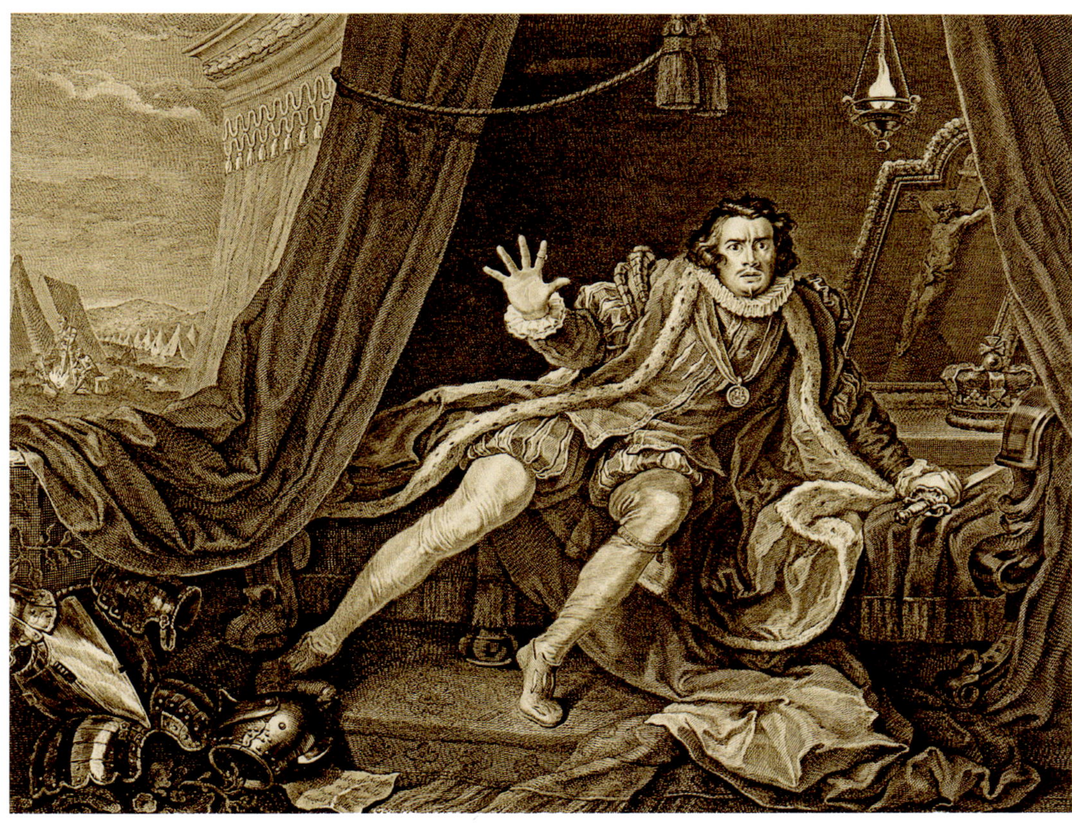

David Garrick playing *Richard III* awakens from his nightmare in the tent near the field of battle, mid-1800s. Etching by W. Hogarth and C. Grignion after W. Hogarth. (Wellcome Collection)

capacity of just over 3,000, and went on to produce pantomimes along with comedies. Sheridan had been backed financially by former banker turned actor Robert Baddeley leaving £100 in his will to provide cake and wine for actors on *Twelfth Night*, a tradition continued ever since.

One of Sheridan's most popular stage performers, and one of Georgian theatre's most famous, was Dorothy Jordan, who held the eye of George III's son and heir, the Duke of Clarence. After George III discovered his son was paying Jordan a considerable amount of money annually, when encountering the duke in Drury Lane's rotunda, much to the surprise of the assembly of theatregoers, the king was seen to box the ears of his son. From that time onwards, the management ensured king and duke were kept apart while attending performances, giving each their own royal box, the only London theatre with one for the reigning sovereign, and one for the Prince of Wales.

Another of Sheridan's actresses, Mrs Sarah Siddons, was born into a family of strolling players, making her name playing the lead role in the tragedy *Isabella* at Drury Lane before going on to receive great acclaim from London's critics when appearing as Volumnia in Shakespeare's *Coriolanus* and her role as Lady Macbeth in the tragedy *Macbeth*. In 1802, the theatre almost became the scene of a real-life tragedy when an assassination attempt was made on the life of George III. From the pit the gunman, James Hadfield, fired two shots from a pistol toward the royal box, missing his target. Hadfield was quickly restrained and taken away. The king, unruffled by the incident, ordered the performance to continue.

Siddons's younger brother, John Kemble, also appeared on stage alongside his sister, performing in several Shakespeare plays and went on to manage Drury Lane for Sheridan, who, by this time, had neglected the theatre after turning to politics, along with turning to heavy drink.

Another troupe of actor siblings, the Bruntons, whose father John Brunton, a Drury Lane grocer turned actor appearing at Covent Garden, was followed onto the stage by son, John, and three of seven daughters, Anne, Elizabeth and Louisa. The four young Brunton siblings had very successful theatrical careers, Louisa collaborating with playwrights Thomas Morton and William Dimond, who created roles for the actress in several of their most popular productions.

After Kemble resigned from his managerial position at Drury Lane, he was appointed manager of its rival at Covent Garden, purchasing a sixth share, a financial outlay that almost forced him into bankruptcy following the theatre burning down. The fire broke out during the night of 19 September 1808, attributed to the discharged wadding of a gun, used during a performance of *Pizarro*, lodging in scenery where it smouldered and caught fire around midnight.

While attempting to put out the blaze, several firemen, the number reported to be between fourteen and twenty-one, were killed when a wall of the theatre collapsed. Actress Harriot Mellon, who lived nearby, ordered a large barrel of ale to sustain the labourers attempting to dig the firemen out, offering £5 for each brought out alive and £2 for the bodies of those who perished. Covent Garden was completely destroyed, along with all the theatre's contents, and if it had not been for the generosity of the patrons raising funds through a public subscription, Kemble would have been ruined financially.

The cost of rebuilding Covent Garden, however, along with the wages to employ a substantial number of staff and stagehands, was far more than estimated, and the

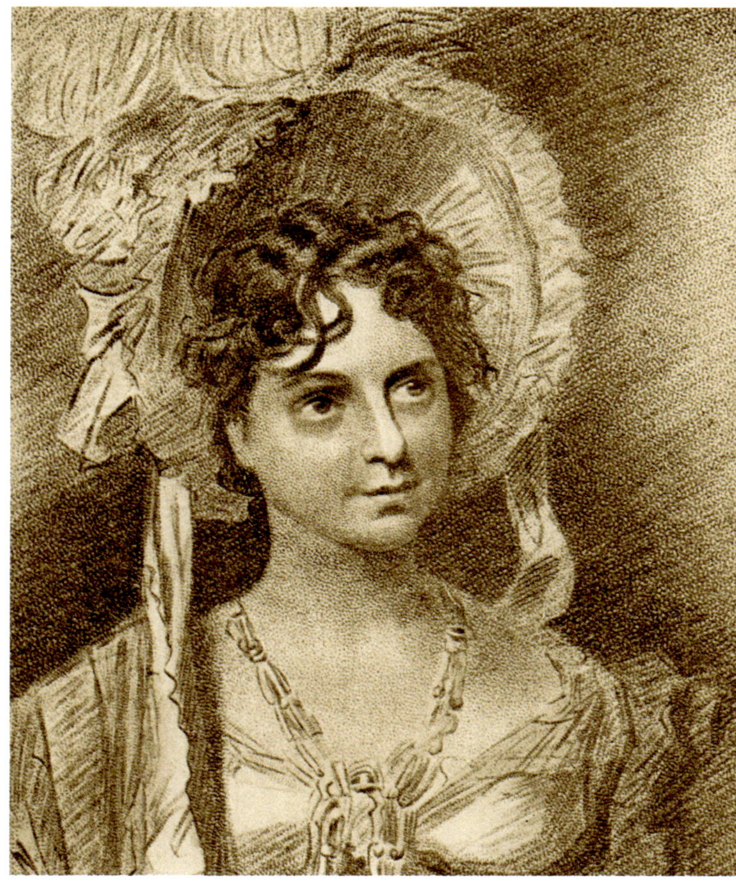

Popular actress during the early eighteenth century, Louisa Brunton, engaged to perform at Covent Garden for £10 per week.

management was forced to increase ticket prices to offset the financial outlay, resulting in a riot breaking out during the opening night performance of *Macbeth*. The theatregoers continued in their protestations and refused to leave the theatre at the end of the performance, Kemble sending for the Bow Street Runners, which made the situation worse, the riot going on into the early hours of the next day.

Known as the Old Price Riots, the protesting continued at performances for over two months until the theatre management backed down and reduced admission prices. This had not been the first time pricing caused disharmony amongst theatregoers; between 1730 and 1780, there were over sixty reported disturbances at London's three major theatres, several resulting in violent actions and wanton damage.

The year after the destruction of Covent Garden, on the night of 24 February 1809, despite the building's acclaimed fire safety precautions, a fierce blaze consumed Drury Lane. Believed to have been caused by an open fire not extinguished in a coffee room when the theatre closed, there was some suspicion the fire might not have been an accident.

Like Covent Garden, everything at Drury Lane was destroyed, the building and all contents, and while the theatre burned, Sheridan, after arriving from a parliamentary debate, calmly went into a nearby tavern, purchased a glass of wine, and strolling back out

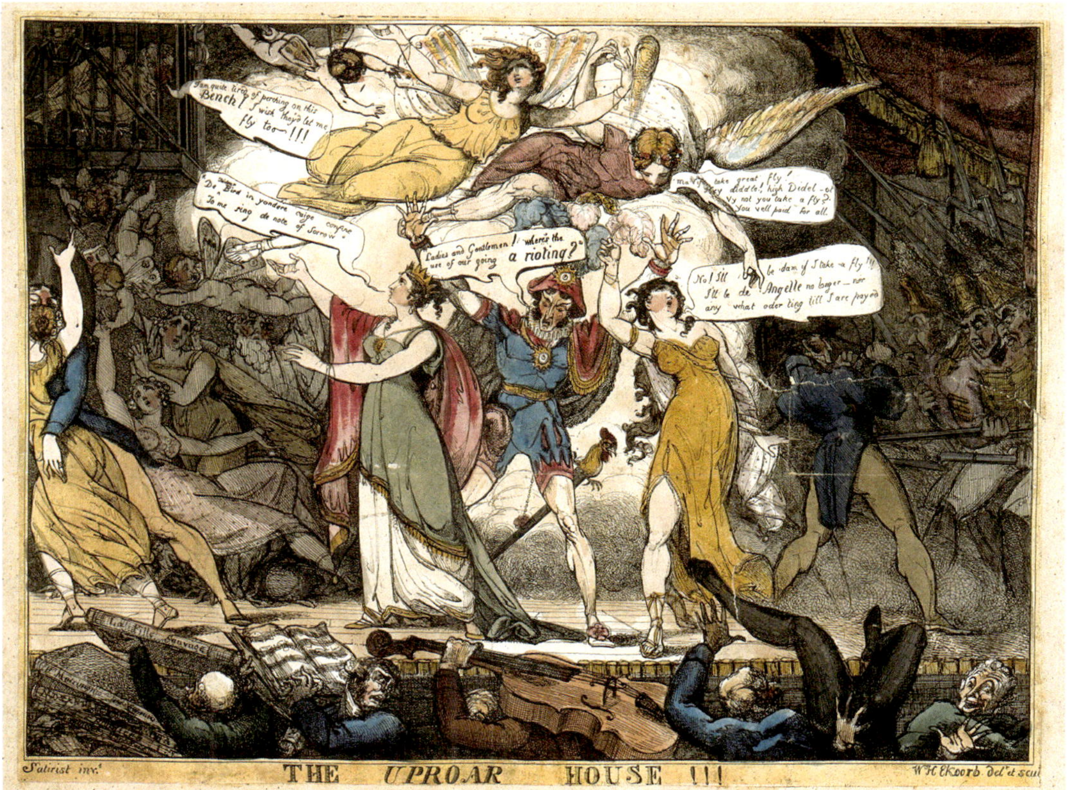

Riot at King's Theatre, Haymarket, May 1813, after singer Catalina refused to perform due to a debt owed by the theatre management. Etching by W. H. Brooke. (Wellcome Collection)

onto the street, glass of wine in hand, was heard to say by astonished onlookers, 'A man may surely be able to take a glass of wine by his own fireside'. Considered a very strange comment to make by a man facing financial ruin, the theatre, insured for £35,000, was estimated to be worth £250,000.

Help was at hand, however, as Sheridan's old friend, brewer Samuel Whitbread, invested a hefty sum in the theatre's rebuild and as head of the theatre committee, eventually took over the company management. Following the theatre's reopening in 1812, Sheridan's involvement ended, and after losing his seat in Parliament, and deep in debt, died in 1816, at a borrowed house on Savile Row.

It is said Drury Lane is the most haunted of all London's theatres. Sightings include a man dressed in grey cloak and tri-corn hat, hinted to be the ghost of a man knifed to death whose skeleton was discovered in 1848, walled up in a small room. The manifestation has been seen on numerous occasions in the upper circle by members of the audience and theatre cleaners. It was also rumoured the ghost was an actor killed by fellow thespian Charles Macklin, after an argument regarding a wig in 1735, or spirit of a country gentleman stabbed to death over a love affair with an actress.

The ghost of Victorian music hall artist Dan Leno occasionally appears in a dressing room, along with an aroma of lavender oil, which Leno often wore. In more recent times,

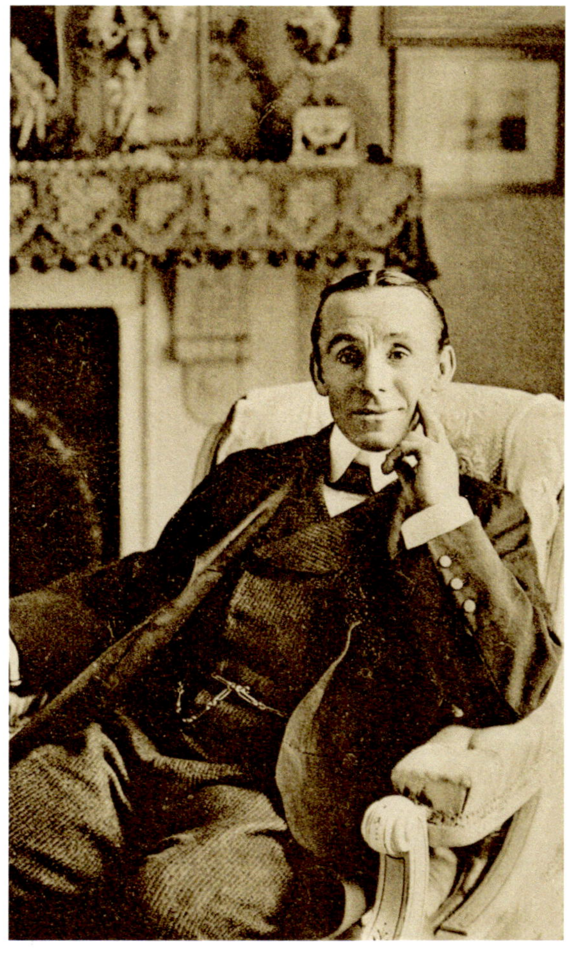

Dan Leno, actor, musical hall comedian and pantomime dame, 1860–1904.

doors slam on their own and actors have witnessed a dressing room television randomly change channels.

At the beginning of the 1800s, while London's legitimate theatre was producing spoken plays along with operas, occasionally entertaining audiences with lion-taming acts and recreated combats on horseback, the capital's ever-increasing population was also able to embrace a variety of theatrical entertainment, musical pantomimes, comedies, melodramas, and operettas, staged at many of London's emerging playhouses. Operators of these theatres were able to apply for a performance licence from a local magistrate, but restricted productions venturing too close to spoken dramatic plays risked prosecution or closure of the theatre.

The major London theatres obtaining such licences included Adelphi on the Strand, originally Sans Pareil founded in 1806 by merchant John Scott and his daughter Jane, who wrote many of the plays performed, and south of the river Astley's Amphitheatre, rebuilt in 1803 after the first burned down, where the world's first circus ring was combined with the stage for large historical battle productions, which even included performing horses.

4

Beginnings of Contemporary Theatre

Throughout the Victorian period, London's theatres faced many changes and challenges. The first major change came in 1843, when the Theatres Act ended the patent theatres' monopoly on producing spoken drama, resulting in many other London theatres competing to attract audiences. The Lord Chamberlain's powers over licensing, which had existed since the mid-1700s, had also been restricted, only permitted to prohibit plays on grounds or morality or public order.

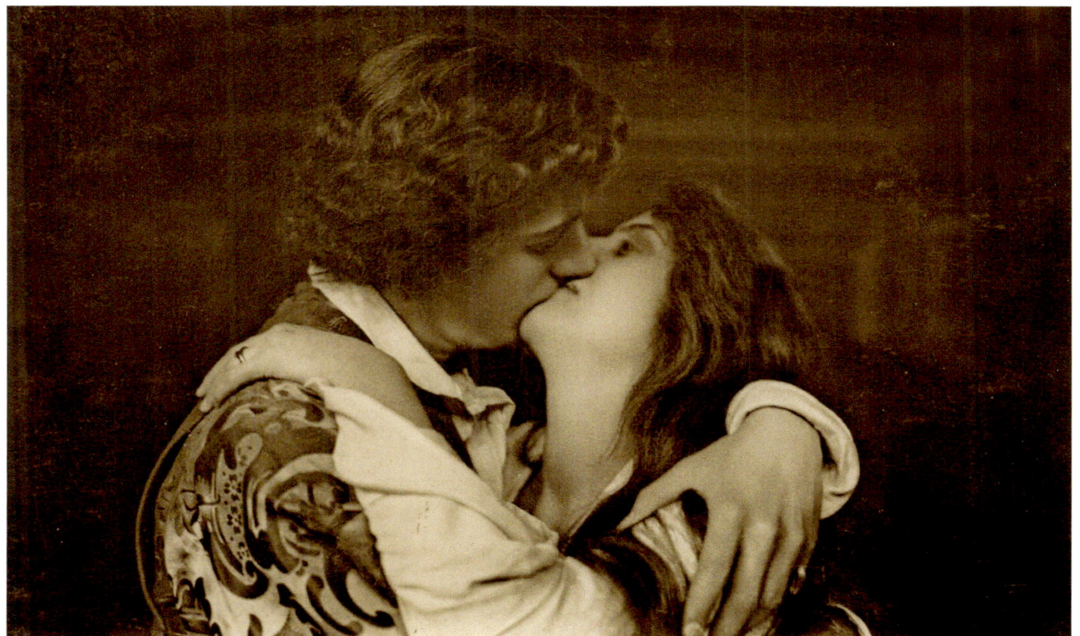

Matheson Lang and Nora Kerin share a passionate embrace performing in Shakespeare's *Romeo and Juliet*, 1908.

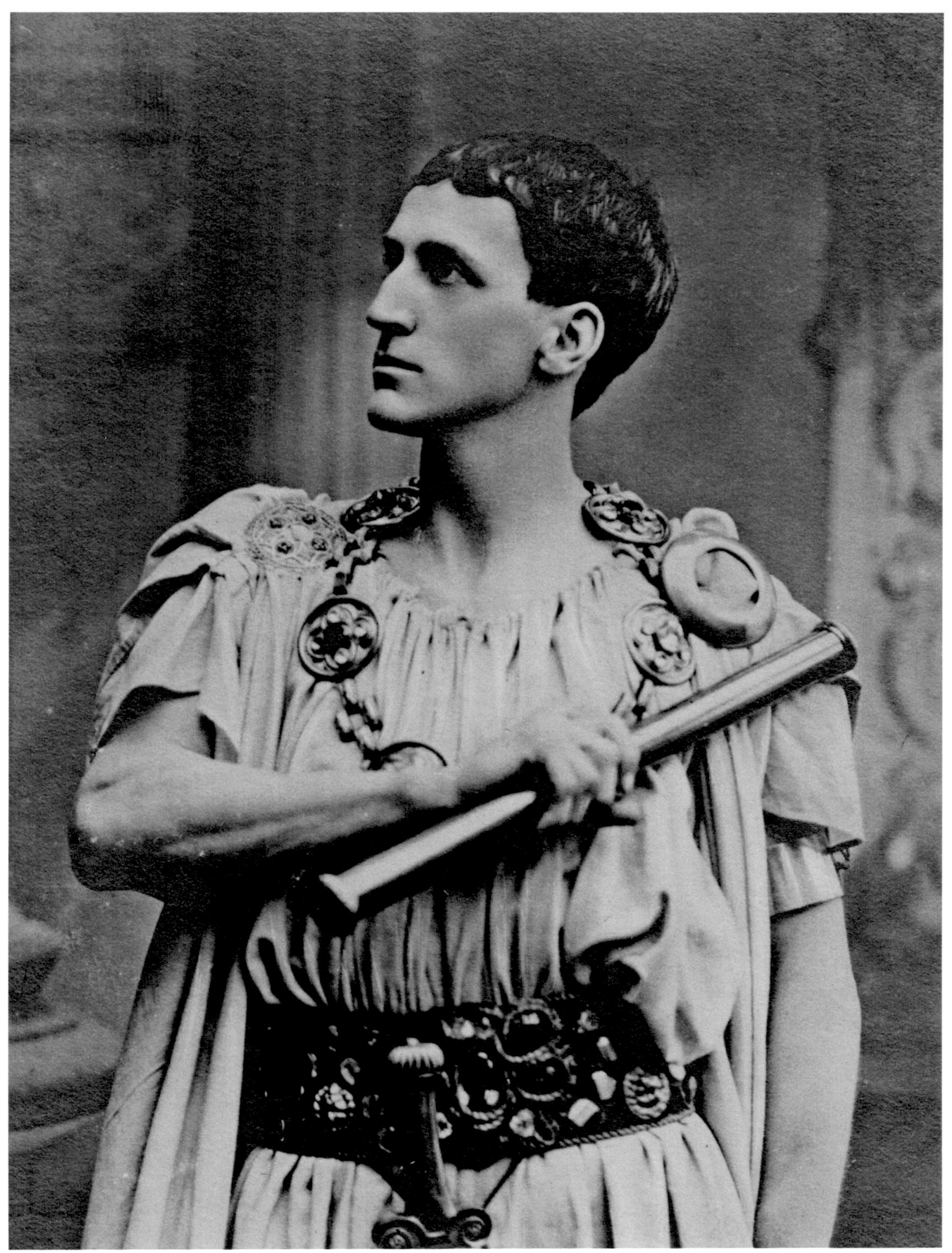

Playing Brutus at Drury Lane in Shakespeare's *Julius Caesar*, budding actor Fred Benson, aged twenty-five, purchased a Shakespeare and classical comedy company in 1883, performing in London and touring throughout Britain.

The relaxing of the licencing laws was primarily in the expectation of providing all members of London's society the prospect of attending more cultured theatrical experiences, and many of Shakespeare's plays were then performed by emerging actors to a much wider audience. It was also expected there would be more opportunities for new playwrights to produce modern dramatic productions; however, a majority were penned based upon historical methods of tried and tested narrative writing, the content featuring historical events which were not always well received.

Many of London's new West End theatres then began staging modern comedies, farces, and thrillers, written by innovative, but poorly paid, up-and-coming playwrights, and with the growth of music halls throughout London, and for the more affluent members of society the opening of the Royal Albert Hall, South Kensington, in 1871, there was a wide variety of entertainment to please Victorian audiences divided by theatrical tastes, social class, and disposable income.

The two original licensed playhouses evolved into two separated musical identities, the Theatre Royal Covent Garden staging opera and ballet, and at Drury Lane's Theatre Royal, spectacular pantomimes were performed alternating with extravagant melodramas. The theatre at Covent Garden was completely refashioned after a fire in 1846, and renamed the Royal Italian Opera, opening with a performance of Rossini's *Semiramide*, the two-act opera based on the life of the legendary waring Queen of Assyria. Just under five years later the theatre burned down after another fire broke out, and was then rebuilt by leading London-based British building company Lucas Brothers, to a design by Edward Middleton Barry, the architect favouring classical styles.

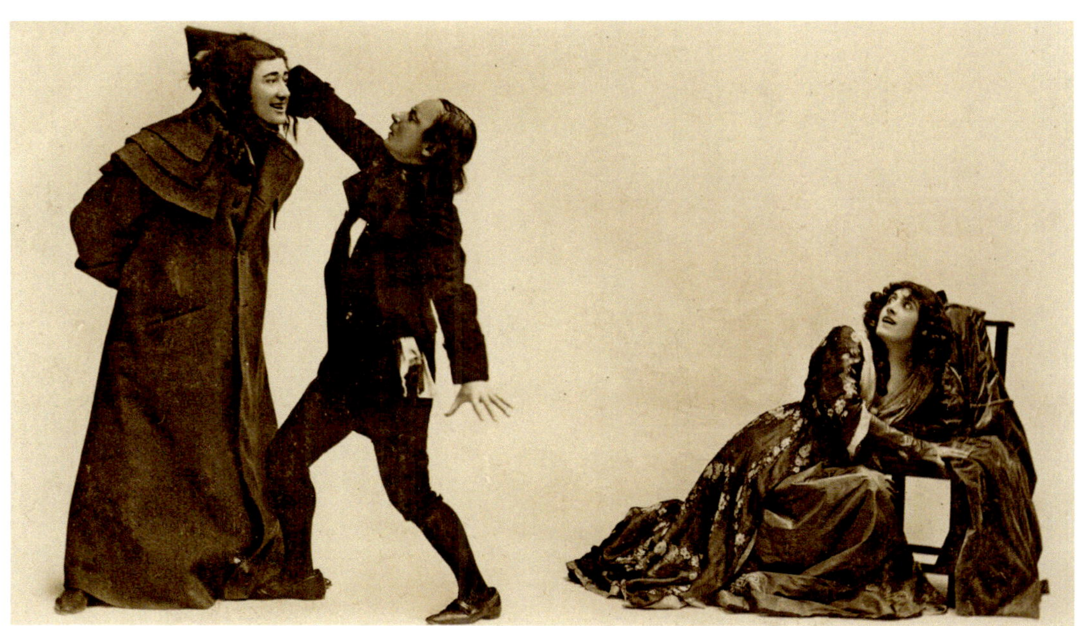

Fred Terry, alongside Horace Hodges and Julia Neilson, is unmasked as the hero and protagonist of a new stage play performed in 1905: *The Scarlet Pimpernel*, an adventure thriller written for the stage by author and playwright Baroness Orczy.

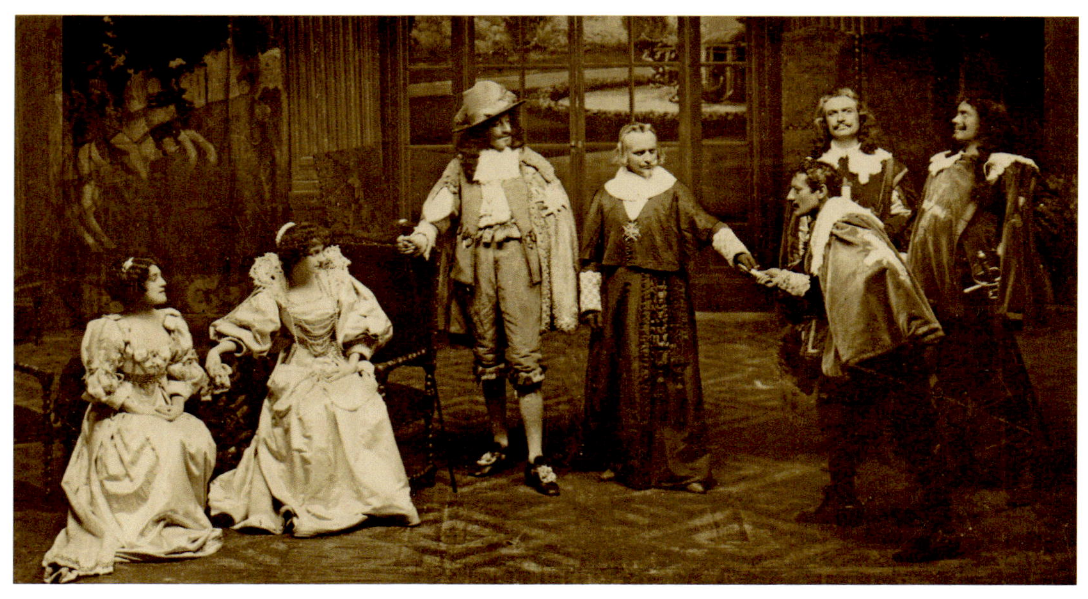

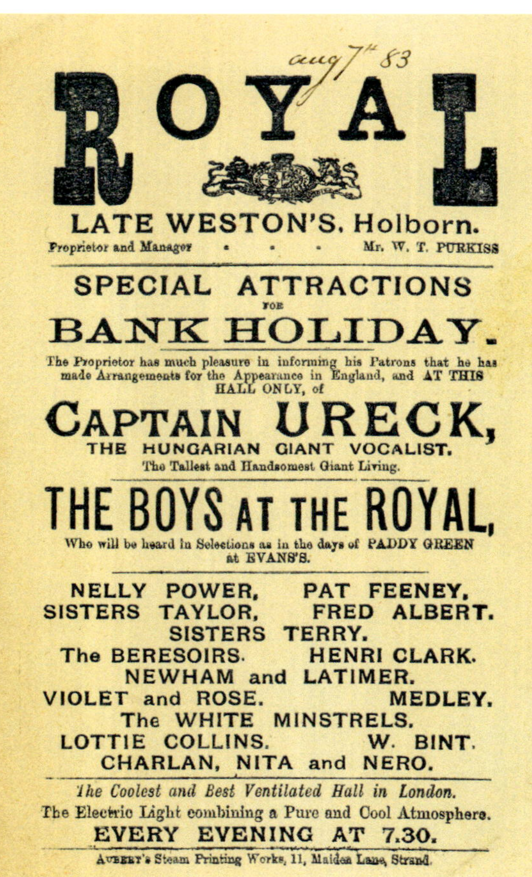

Above: Third from right, actor Lewis Waller's representation of D'Artagnan in the 1989 stage adaptation of *The Three Musketeers* made him into a stage idol. Waller appeared with Madge Titheradge, Evelyn D'Alroy, Gayer Mackay, A. E. George, Bassett Roe and Herbert Jarman.

Left: Formerly Weston's Music Hall, this poster advertises variety acts appearing at the Royal, August 1883.

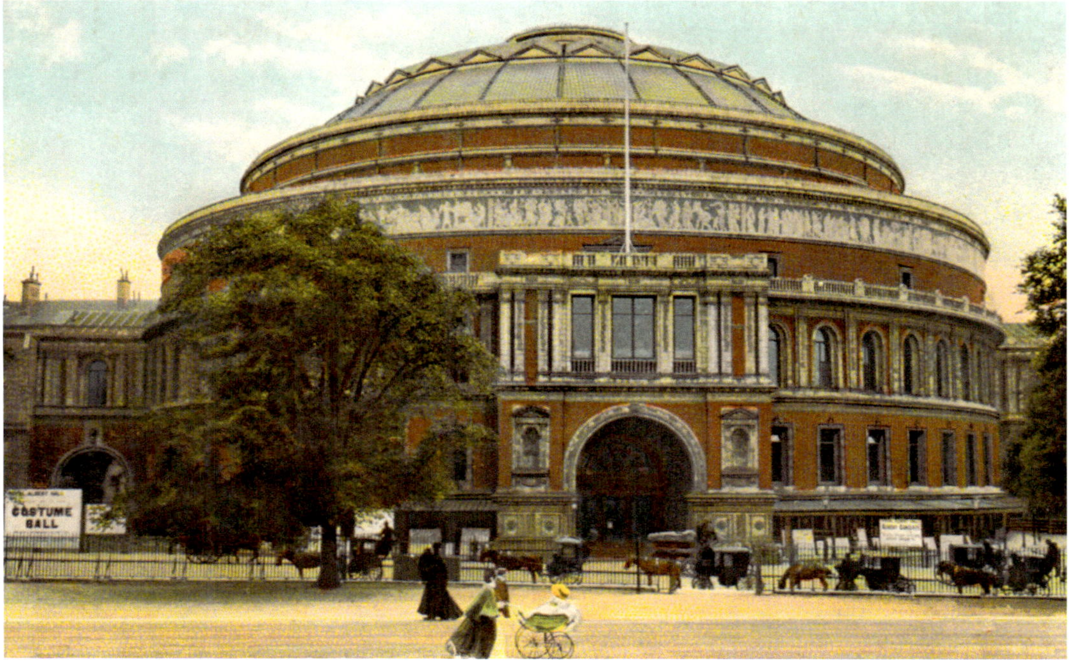

Royal Albert Hall, opened by Queen Victoria in 1871, named to commemorate her late husband, Prince Albert.

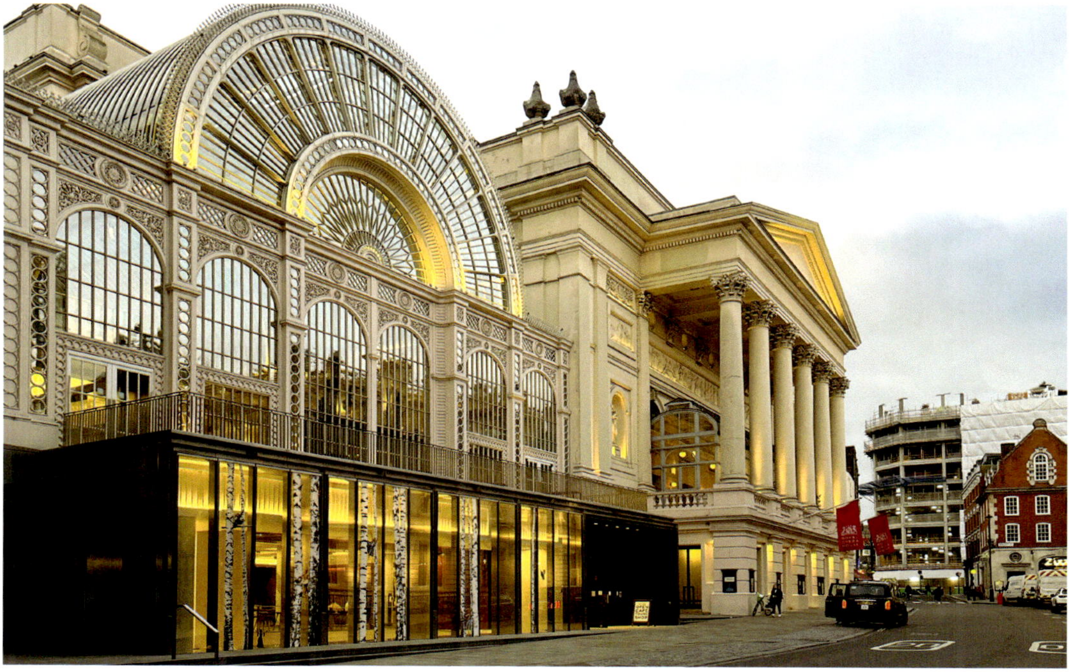

Royal Opera House, Bow Street, Covent Garden.

Over the years Covent Garden was extended and improved. Then, after the Royal English Opera company took up residence, the theatre was renamed the Royal Opera House.

The Christmas pantomimes staged at Drury Lane, the first starring comedian Dan Leno in 1888, were huge financial successes. The former traditional Italian-based productions from which British pantomime evolved had gradually developed into what theatregoers today would recognise as slapstick comedy, with expanded plotlines taken from folk tales and fairy stories with the inclusion of musical numbers.

Staged dramatic productions also evolved, becoming ever more spectacular, with fantastic innovative effects included to enhance the theatregoer's experience such as a working paddle steamer, a recreated train crash, and real horses racing on a treadmill.

While both former licenced theatres drew in huge attendances, London's smaller venues were also flourishing in their freedom to stage varying productions of classical dramas, melodramas, operettas, musicals, comedies, and farce. From the mid-1800s, many new theatres were built, while those existing were either refurbished or reconstructed to accommodate the multitude of theatregoers travelling into London from all across the country, as well as from overseas, eager to be entertained at a theatrical spectacle.

Wherever you journey throughout London, you will find a theatre or performance space close by, and although the area of Drury Lane and Covent Garden is recognised as the place where Renaissance theatre evolved at both the Theatre Royal and the Royal Opera House, the only existing theatre actually on Drury Lane, the New London Theatre, was not built

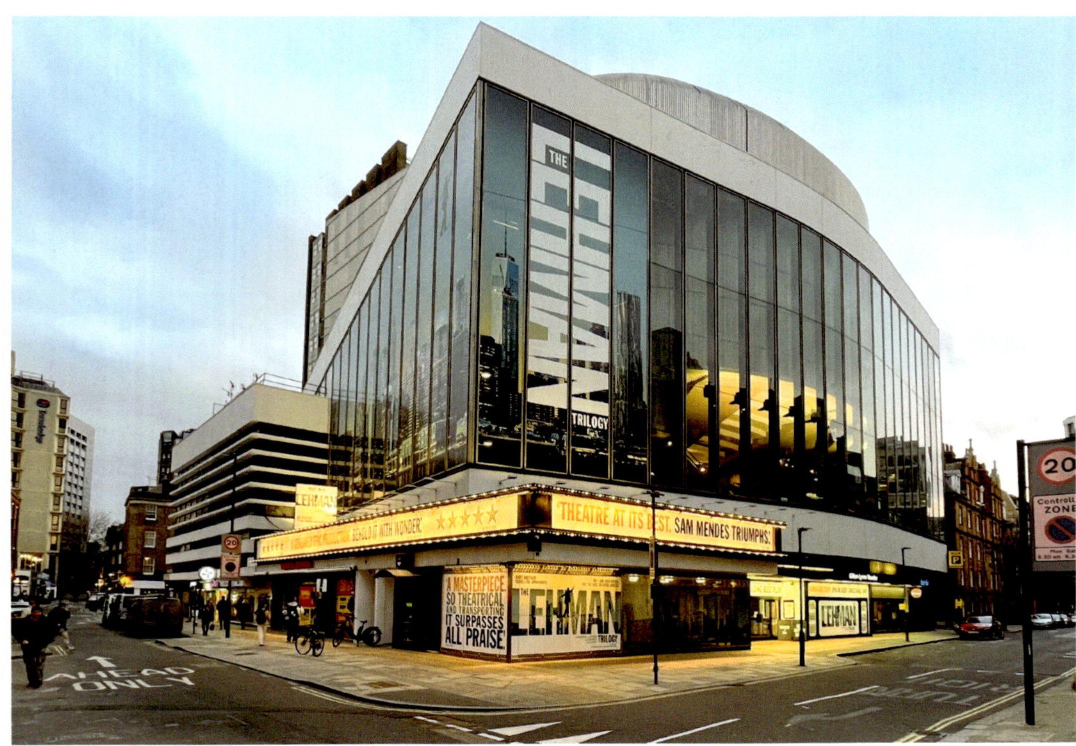

Gillian Lynne Theatre complex on Drury Lane.

until the mid-twentieth century, officially opening on 10 January 1973 with *The Unknown Soldier and his Wife* staring Peter Ustinov.

Erected as part of a large building project to include apartments, shops and restaurant, the glass-panel clad complex, designed by Croatian architect Paul Tvrtkovic, was situated on the site of a music hall and later Winter Garden Theatre, demolished in 1965.

Prior to New London Theatre's opening, actress and singer Marlene Dietrich performed two concerts in November 1972, recorded by the BBC. The theatre house was remarkable in design as the stage, orchestra pit, and front section of the stalls revolve, and when lights and walls were raised automatically, the theatre transformed into an amphitheatre seating an audience of over 900. In June 2018, the theatre was renamed the Gillian Lynne Theatre, in memory of the choreographer of several award-winning musicals, including Andrew Lloyd Webber's *Cats*, first staged at the theatre in 1981, which ran for a record-breaking 8,949 performances over seventeen years.

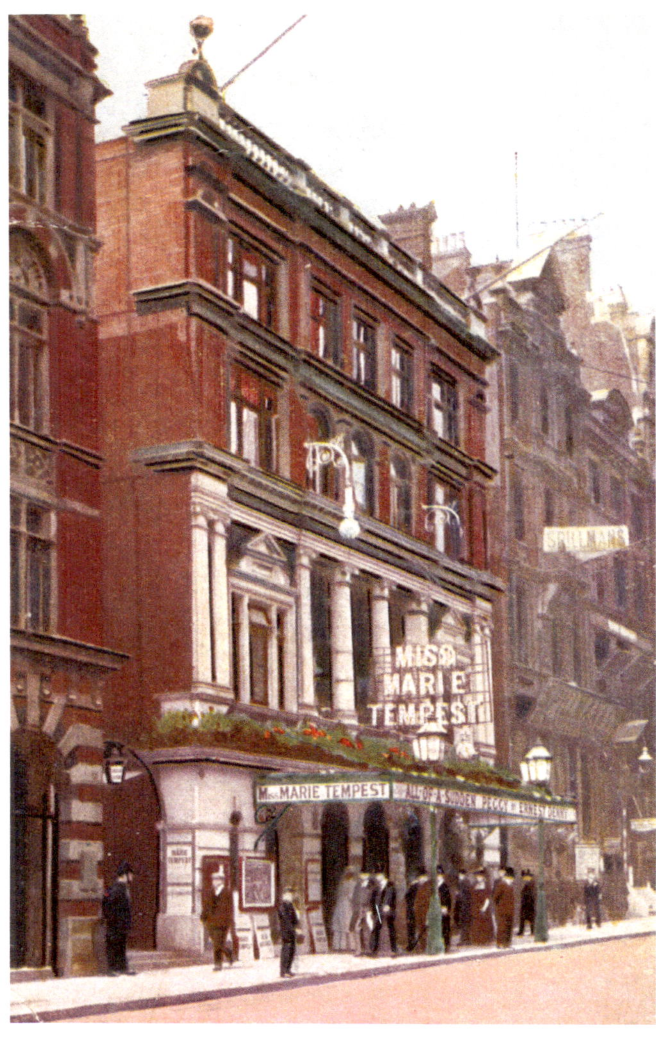

Duke of York's Theatre,
St Martin's Lane, early 1900s.

As London's theatreland grew, St Martin's Lane was becoming a fashionable and popular area of the West End, with large mansion houses, an art academy, coffee houses, shops, and public houses along its route, and narrow lanes running off on each side. Opposite the sixteenth-century pedestrian walkthrough, Goodwins Court, is the first theatre built on St Martin's Lane, The Duke of York's, designed by architect Walter Emden for actor, playwright, and theatre manager Frank Wyatt and his wife, actress and theatre manager Violet Melnotte.

Opening in 1892 as the Trafalgar Square Theatre, the first production was a comic opera, *The Wedding Eve*, by French composer Frédéric Toulmouche. Two years later the theatre was renamed The Duke of York's in honour of future King George V, where in 1904 audiences witnessed a boy fly for the first time in the production of J. M. Barrie's magical *Peter Pan, or the Boy Who Wouldn't Grow Up*. Starring Nina Boucicault in the title role, Captain Jas Hook was played by Gerald De Maurier, the father of three daughters, authors Angela and Daphne and artist Jeanne. Grade II listed in 1960, The Duke of York's underwent refurbishment in the late 1970s.

To the south of St Martin's Lane, erected at the beginning of the twentieth century is the London Coliseum, at the time London's most luxurious theatre of variety designed by architect Frank Matcham, and with 2,359 seats, the largest in the capital. One of the first to have electric lighting on stage, after a long succession of variety productions, musical comedies, plays, and pantomime performances, as well as a cricket match played between Middlesex and Surrey in 1907, the theatre was converted into a cinema in the mid-1960s.

Restored as a theatre when the Sadler's Wells Opera Company moved in, the Coliseum also played host to The English Royal Ballet. One of the most popular and frequently performed operas ever written, *Carmen* by Georges Bizet, has been staged on several occasions at the London Coliseum, most recently by the English National Opera. The Edwardian theatre, with its baroque interior design and luxuriously decorated house, was Grade II listed by English Heritage in 1960, and is still considered today as one of London's grandest theatres.

The area of St Martin's accommodates several theatres, including Ambassadors and St Martin's, both designed by acclaimed theatre architect W. G. Sprague. It was planned for both to be constructed as companions to each other on West Street, just off Monmouth Street. Ambassadors was completed in 1913, but due to the outbreak of the First World War, the construction of St Martin's was delayed by three years.

Unlike other theatres built around the same period, Ambassadors was intended to be an intimate, smaller venue, decorated in a style known as Louis XVI, with a seating capacity of just under 450. St Martin's had a slightly larger capacity of 550. Early performances included mostly musicals and dramatic plays, as well as one of the first sci-fi productions, *R.U.R.*, in 1923, starring Basil Rathbone. Written by Czech playwright Karel Čapek, the play's title was an acronym of *Rossumovi Univerzální Roboti,* from where the name 'robot' originated.

Following a succession of successful plays, in 1974, Agatha Christie's murder mystery *The Mousetrap* transferred the short distance from Ambassadors to St Martin's Lane, where the play went on to break all records for the longest continuously running show of all time. However, like other productions throughout London's theatreland, performances were halted in March 2020, during the Covid pandemic lockdown, the play reopening just over a year later in May 2021.

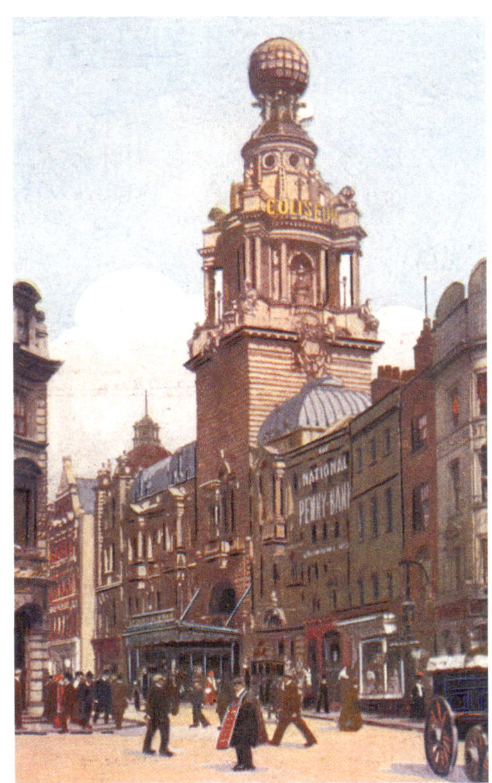

London Coliseum, St Martin's Lane,
early 1900s.

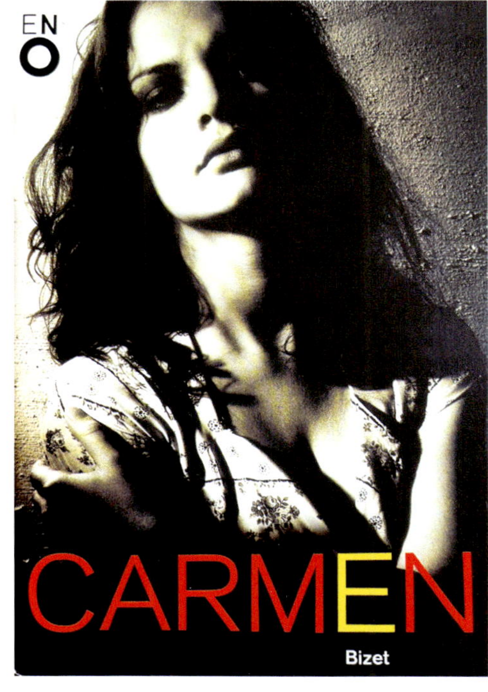

Programme for ENO's production of Bizet's
Carmen, 2001.

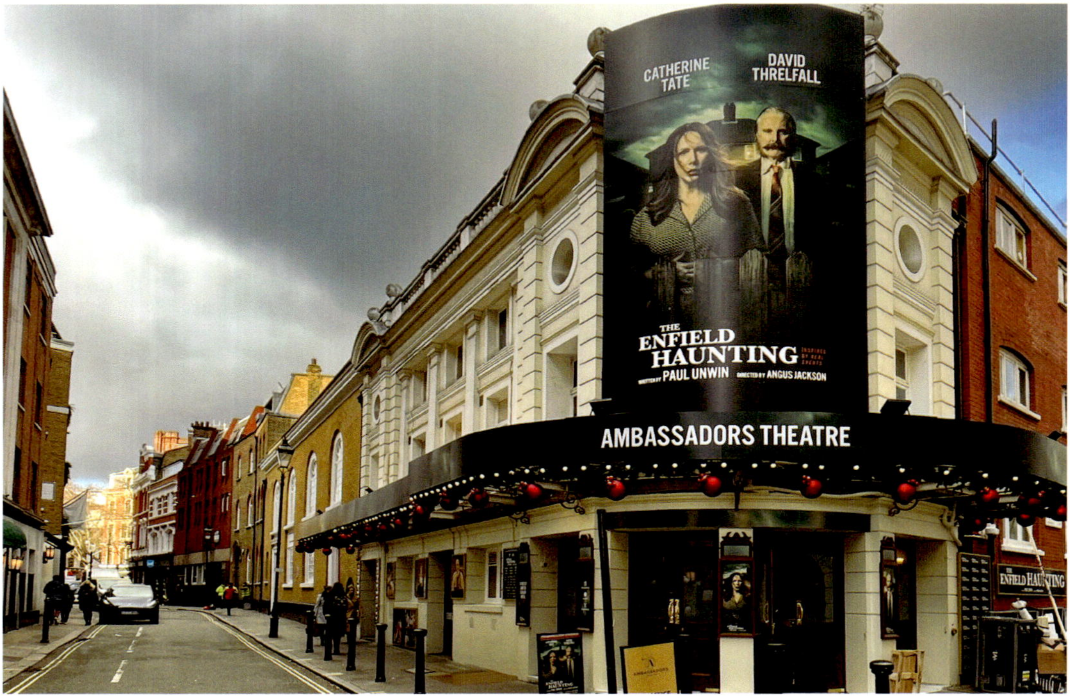

Ambassadors Theatre, West Street.

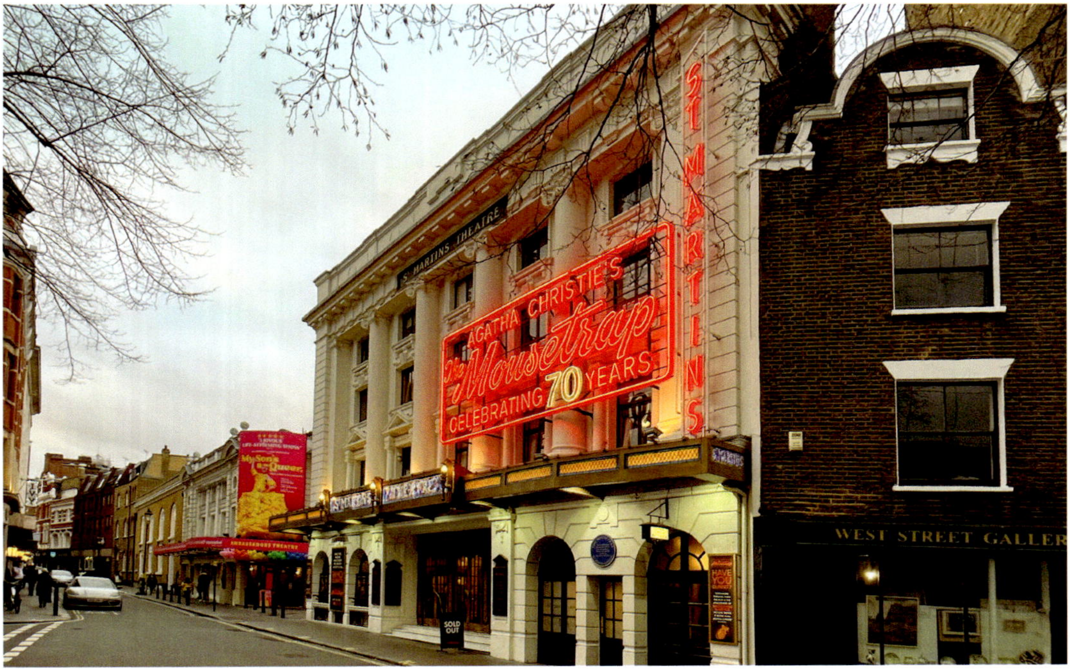

St Martin's Lane Theatre celebrating the 70th Anniversary Tour of *The Mousetrap*, 2023.

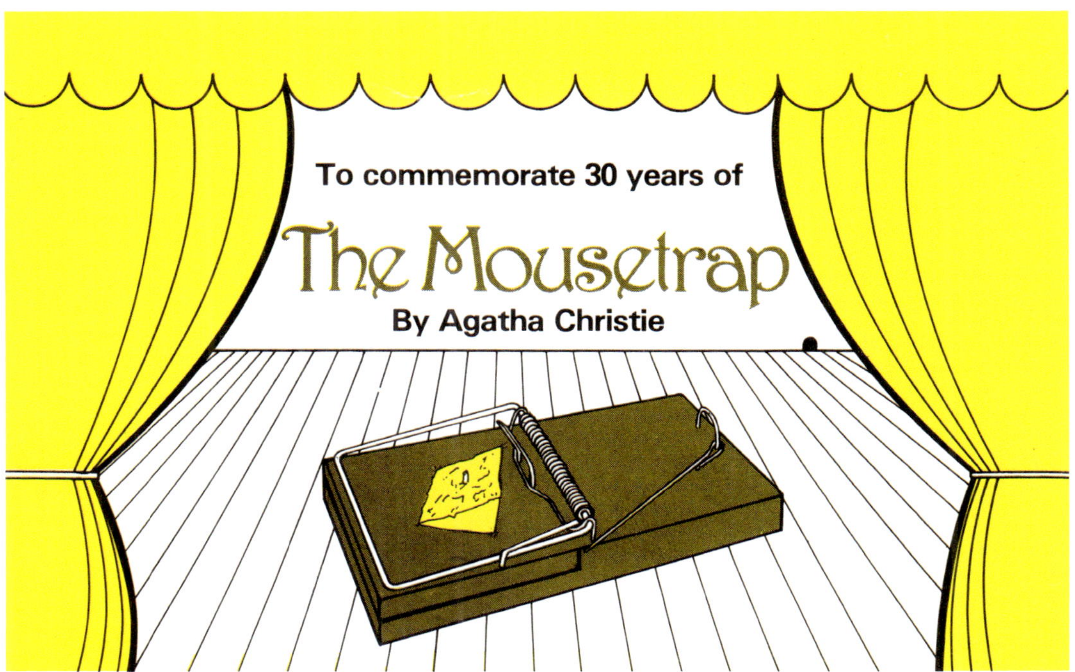

One of 1,000 limited edition postcards produced for the 30th Anniversary of *The Mousetrap* opening in London.

It was intended for St Martin's to have been named the Irving Theatre, after actor-manager Sir Henry Irving, the first actor to receive a knighthood, and whose statue had been erected on the grounds of the National Portrait Gallery at the junction of St Martin's Lane and Charing Cross Road in 1910.

Somerset-born Irving, after treading the boards in the north of England and Scotland, came to critical acclaim in 1871, appearing at the London Lyceum in a production of *The Bells*. Irving played the lead role of Mathias, the burgomaster of Alsace, the character tormented by his past indiscretions involving robbery and murder.

The success of *The Bells* brought the actor many other important roles in a succession of classical productions and revival plays, especially those of Shakespeare; his portrayals of Wolsey in *Henry VIII*, Shylock in *The Merchant of Venice,* and the title roles in *Othello, Macbeth,* and *King Lear* singled Irving out as the most accomplished actor of his day. In 1878, Irving, in partnership with actress Ellen Terry, took over the management of the Lyceum where both appeared on stage performing a succession of Shakespeare plays.

The original Lyceum was located on the north of the Strand, built as an exhibition centre of entertainment, which included a circus and waxworks, along with holding bare-knuckle boxing matches. Converted into a theatre by Samuel Arnold in 1794, when refused a licence after objections by the managers of neighbouring Patent theatres, the Lyceum became home to a series of panoramic scenes of important historic events. After Drury Lane burned down, its company relocated to the Lyceum, which became a theatre in its own right, up until it was also destroyed by fire in 1830.

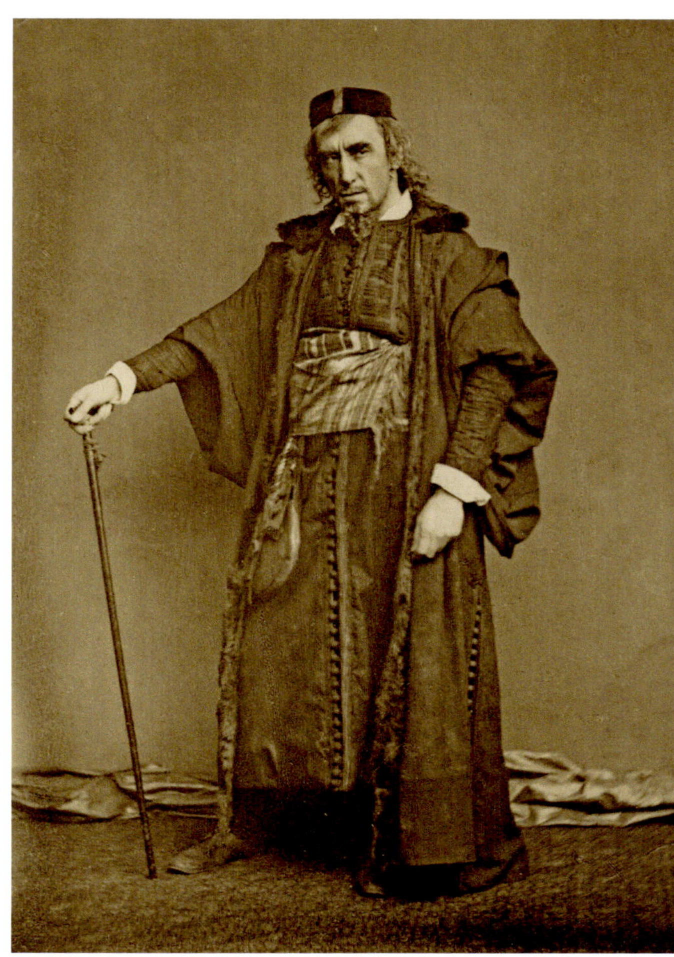

Sir Henry Irving portrays Shylock in the production of *The Merchant of Venice*, 1888.

Rebuilt to a design by Samuel Beazley, north of the original site, the main entrance located on present-day Wellington Street, the theatre opened in 1834, named Theatre Royal Lyceum and English Opera House. Although various alterations and refurbishments were carried out during the following fifty years, the Lyceum was rebuilt in 1904, retaining the theatre's façade and portico main entrance. Refurbished as a cinema in 1937, after only one film showing, due to cinematic rights of distribution, the Lyceum reverted to a theatre until converted into a ballroom at the end of the Second World War.

Successful as an entertainment venue for ballroom dances and cabaret – Miss World contests were held there from 1951 to 1968 – the Lyceum hosted musical concerts, where many popular artists of their day appeared, including Bob Marley, The Who, Led Zeppelin, Pink Floyd, and The Clash. The theatre was also used on many occasions for television broadcasts. Although Grade II listed, the Lyceum's future was in jeopardy when it fell into a state of dilapidation after closure in 1985. The Lyceum was restored in 1996 as a theatre for modern musical operas, including the long-running musical *The Lion King*, first performed in 1999.

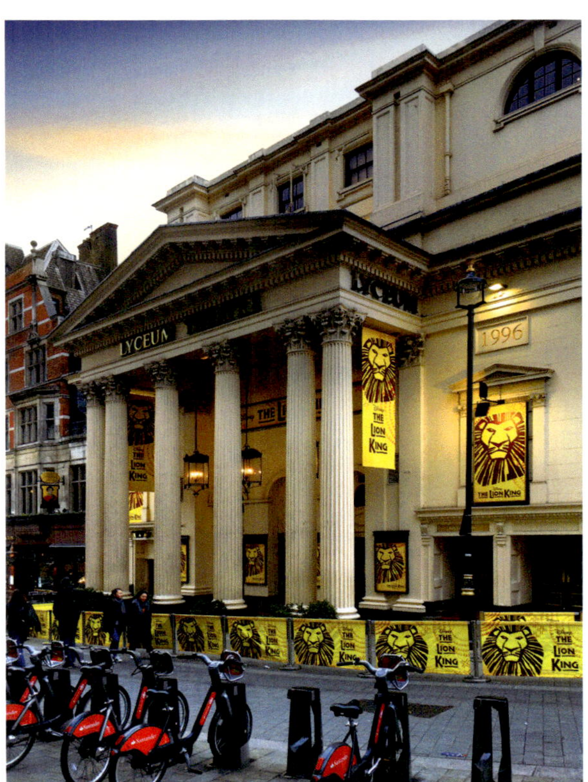

Lyceum where *The Lion King* opened in 1999, running for more than 7,500 performances.

Situated north of the Lyceum and to the south of Theatre Royal are a cluster of theatres on the edge of Aldwych, a crescent-shaped route created in the early 1900s, after existing streets along with four theatres, Olympic, Opera Comique, Globe, and Gaiety, were all demolished. With Aldwych under construction, a new Gaiety Theatre was built, opening with a performance of *The Orchid* in October 1903, attended by King Edward VII and Queen Alexandra. The theatre was host to a series of popular musical comedies until its closure leading up to the Second World War and planned demolition for further road reconstruction.

Although the war halted the theatre's destruction along with the proposed road development, struck by a bomb during the Blitz, the Gaiety was eventually demolished in 1957. Other theatres built at the time of the Aldwych regeneration fared much better.

The Waldorf Theatre, erected in 1905, was part of an elegant stone-built development with the exclusive Waldorf Hotel at the centre and Aldwych Theatre at the far end, designed in the Edwardian baroque style by W. G. R. Sprague. The entrance and frontage of each theatre were identical.

The lavish and luxurious Waldorf Theatre interior was designed in the style of Louis XIV, adorned with splendid decorative marble and plaster features, with a seating capacity of just over 1,000. Opening with a series of Italian operas, after a change of management the theatre was renamed the Strand. Purchased by American F. C. Whitney, the owner and manager changed the name to the Whitney Theatre; however, after his unsuccessful

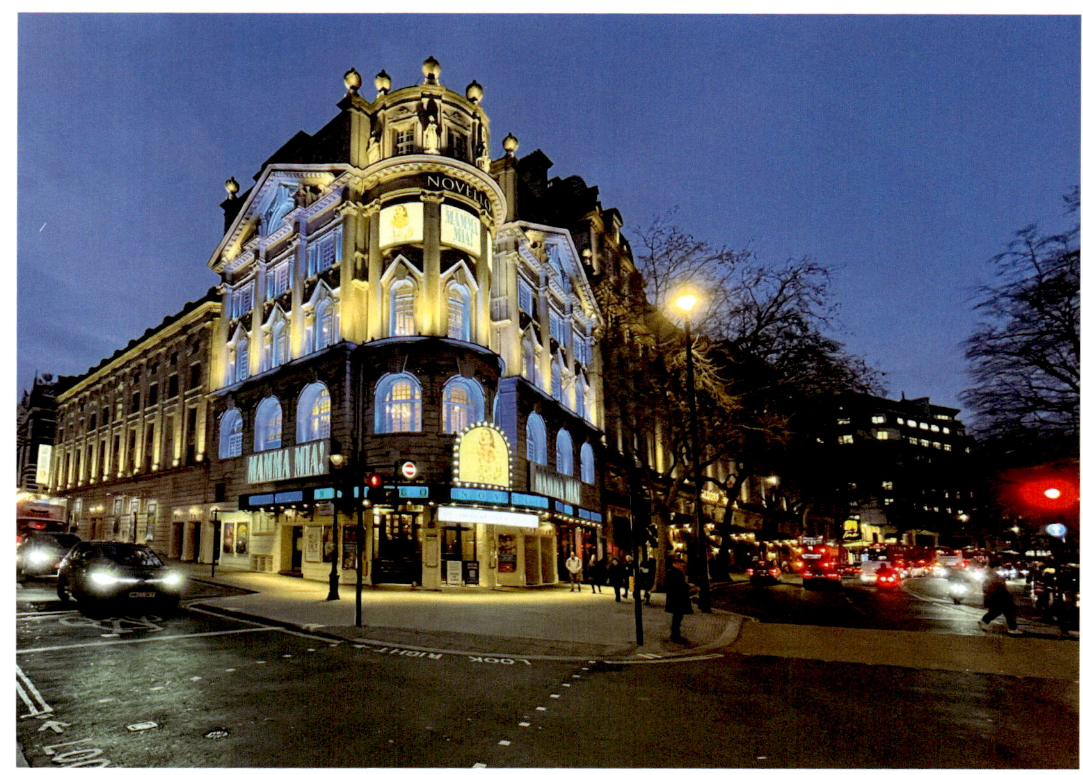

Novello Theatre, formerly the Waldorf, one of a pair of theatres built on the Aldwych.

short theatrical venture, the name reverted to the Strand. Suffering damage from bombs dropped by a zeppelin during the First World War, the theatre was partly reconstructed and refurbished during the 1930s.

To celebrate the theatre's centenary in 2005, after being acquired by the Delfont Mackintosh group, owned by theatre impresario Bernard Delfont and producer Cameron Mackintosh, the Strand was renamed the Novello, after actor, dramatist, and singer Ivor Novello, who resided in a flat above the theatre between 1913 and 1951, from where he composed many popular songs and musicals.

At the opposite end of the development, Aldwych Theatre opened in December 1905 with the pantomime *Blue Bell* and became recognised for a series of twelve farces performed continuously between 1923 and 1933, known as Aldwych Farces, all but three written by Ben Travers. Many of the farces were later made into films and television productions.

In 1949, Laurance Olivier, who along with contemporaries John Gielgud and Ralph Richardson were all predominant on the London stage, directed his wife, Vivien Leigh, in the first London production of Tennessee William's *A Streetcar Named Desire* at The Aldwych, Leigh playing Blanche DuBois.

With references to homosexuality and promiscuity, along with a scene involving rape, the bold production, although attracting much controversy, was a commercial success, and Leigh's commanding performance ensured she would go on to reprise the role in the

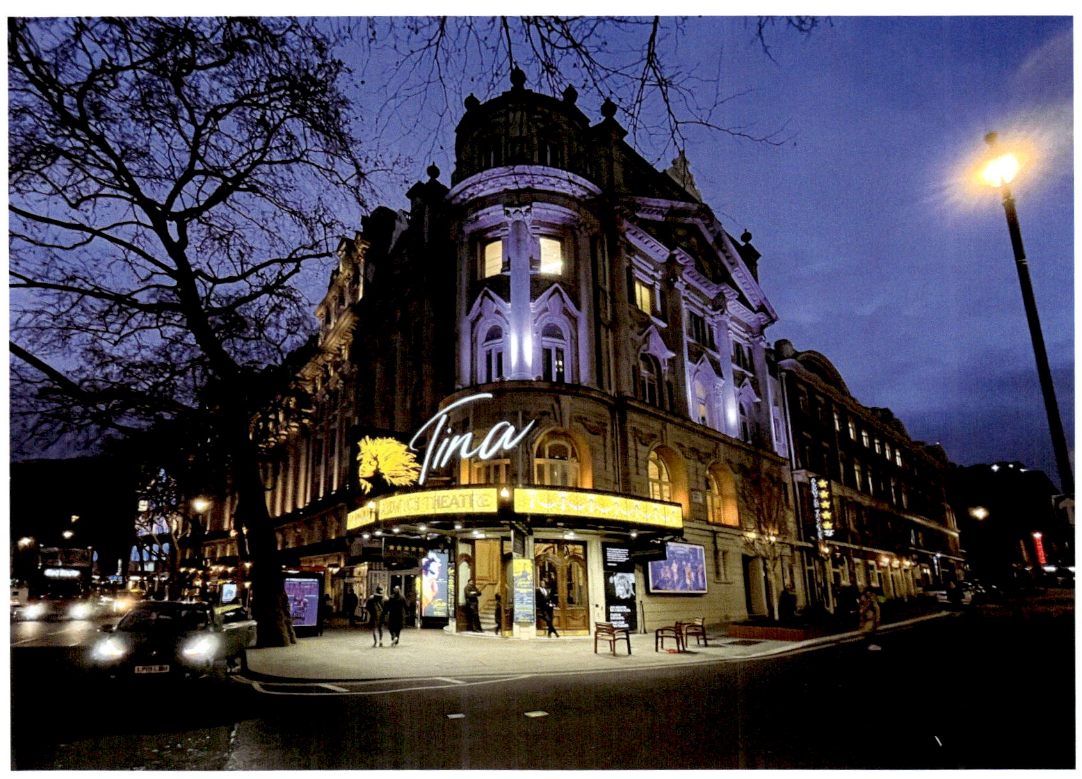

Aldwych Theatre, the frontage matching that of the Novello.

American-made film version of the play released in 1952. The day after Vivien Leigh died from tuberculosis on 8 July 1967, the lights of all theatres in central London were turned off for an hour as a mark of respect.

To the south of Aldwych, an area bombed by the same zeppelin, which had dropped a bomb on the Gaiety Theatre, a site had been left vacant due to planning regulations preventing any proposed new buildings from blocking the light of its neighbours. In 1927, architect Ewen Barr overcame this ruling by designing a theatre on the irregularly shaped site with the upper stories set back from the subterranean built stalls and the box office and foyer situated snuggly below a single steeply racked balcony.

One of London's smaller theatres, the interior was well laid out and every space was used efficiently. The style of the theatre's outer stone façade was described at the time as modern Tudor Gothic, the main entrance opening onto Catherine Street. Because of the depth of the theatre's house below ground level, water continually seeped into the basement, and bilge pumps were installed to regularly pump out the water.

Named the Duchess, the theatre opened on 29 November 1929 with the production *Tunnel Trench*, by Hubert Griffith, who served with the Royal Fusiliers in the First World War. His play featured military service during the conflict, extremely appropriate considering the theatre was erected on a First World War bombsite. In 1930, a production, *The Intimate Revue*, set a shortest-run record on the London stage at the Duchess, lasting

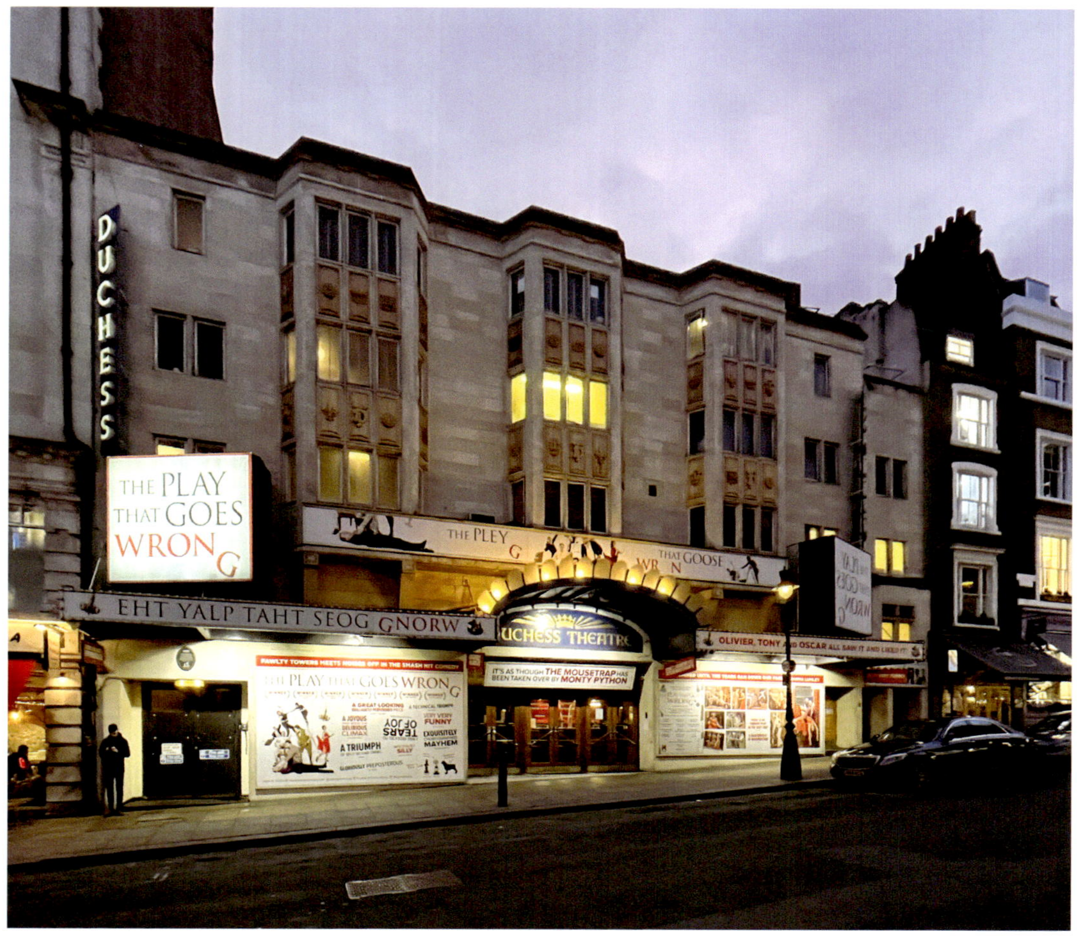

Duchess Theatre, Catherine Street.

no longer than a single performance, many members of the audience walking out before the curtain came down. Although returning to the Duchess under a revised name, the play's second run lasted only two weeks.

The first theatre in London built after the First World War, the Fortune, was erected on the site of a public house, the Albion Tavern at Russell Street, close to where the famous Cockpit playhouse once stood. Financed by Laurence Cowen, who wrote the Fortune's opening night play, *Sinners*, performed on 8 November 1924, the theatre's designer, Ernest Schaufelberg, also designed the Adelphi Theatre on the Strand. The bronze nude installed high up on the Fortune's modernist Italianate concrete façade, Terpsichore, a Greek goddess of dance, was sculptured by M. H. Crichton, a member of the Bromsgrove Guild.

Hosting performances by ENSA during the Second World War, the public enthusiastically eager to be entertained even while suffering air raids, the Fortune became a receiving house, a theatre that hosted touring companies rather than producing its own repertoire. With a seating capacity of only 432, the Fortune is believed to be the second smallest theatre in London's West End.

48

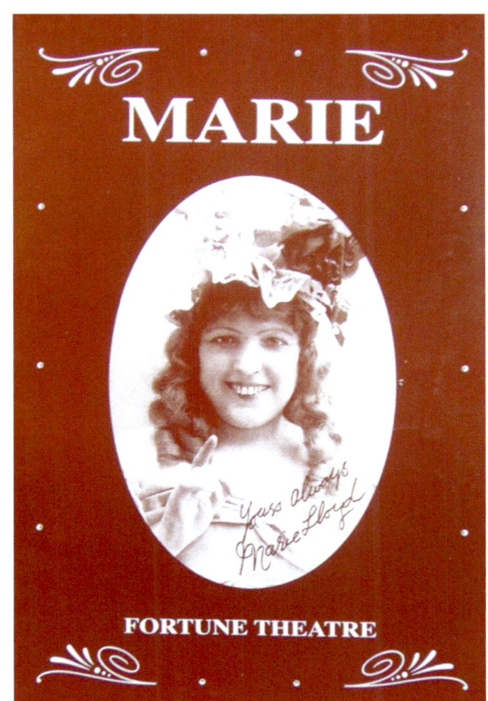

Right: Programme from *Marie*, musical dedicated to music hall star Marie Lloyd, played by Elizabeth Mansfield, the Fortune Theatre, 1995.

Below: Fortune Theatre, Russell Street.

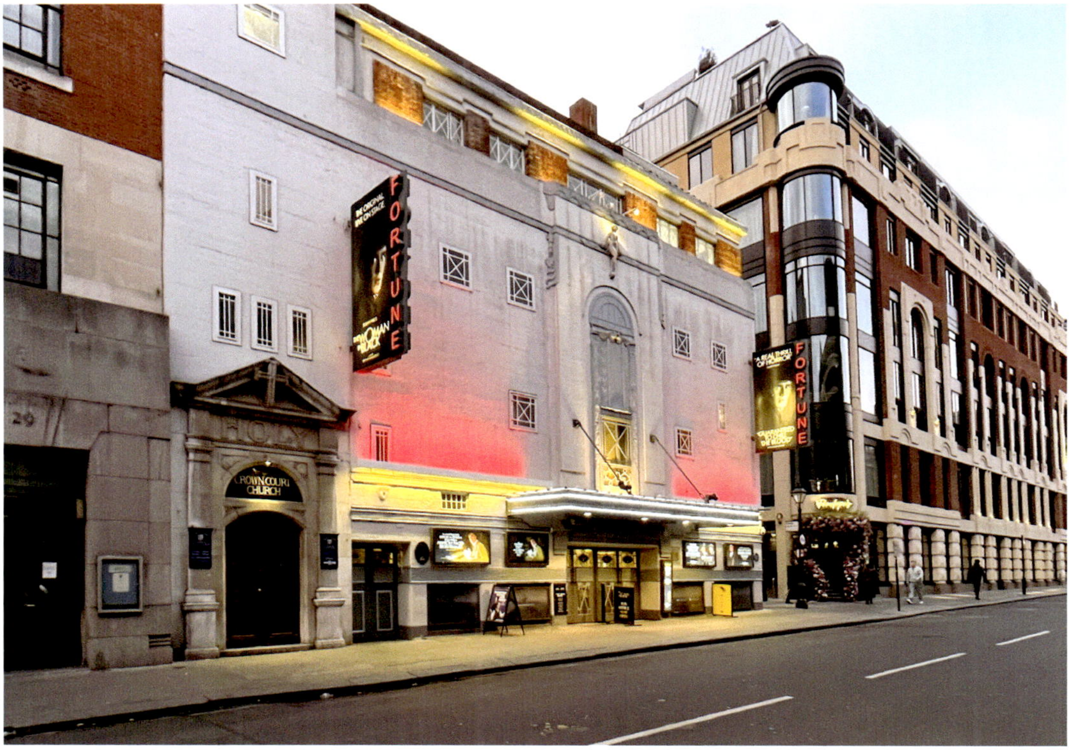

The Adelphi Theatre on the Strand was not the first to occupy the site; the first theatre, Sans Pareil, was opened in 1806 by local tradesman John Scott, specifically to launch the acting career of his daughter Jane, who went on to become a successful actress, theatre manager and playwright. Sold in 1819, the theatre was renamed the Adelphi after a large riverside residence. The theatre became well known for staging a series of melodramas, known as Adelphi Screamers.

Renamed Theatre Royal Adelphi, a new façade was added before the theatre was rebuilt in 1858. Under the ownership of restaurateur Carlo Gatti, after purchasing adjoining properties, including three inns, the theatre was enlarged, renovated, and refurbished with the addition of a restaurant. Completely rebuilt in 1901, to the design of Ernest Runtz, the theatre was reopened as the Century Theatre, but soon reverted to the Adelphi, home to a series of musical comedies up until reconstructed thirty years later.

Although retaining parts of the previous theatre's structure, the house, foyers, and façade were completely rebuilt in the art deco style, reopening on 8 December 1930 with the musical production *Ever Green*. Purchased by Andrew Lloyd Webber's Really Useful Group in 1993, the Adelphi went through a complete refurbishment before opening with the musical *Sunset Boulevard*, the music written by Webber and lyrics by Don Black and Christopher Hampton.

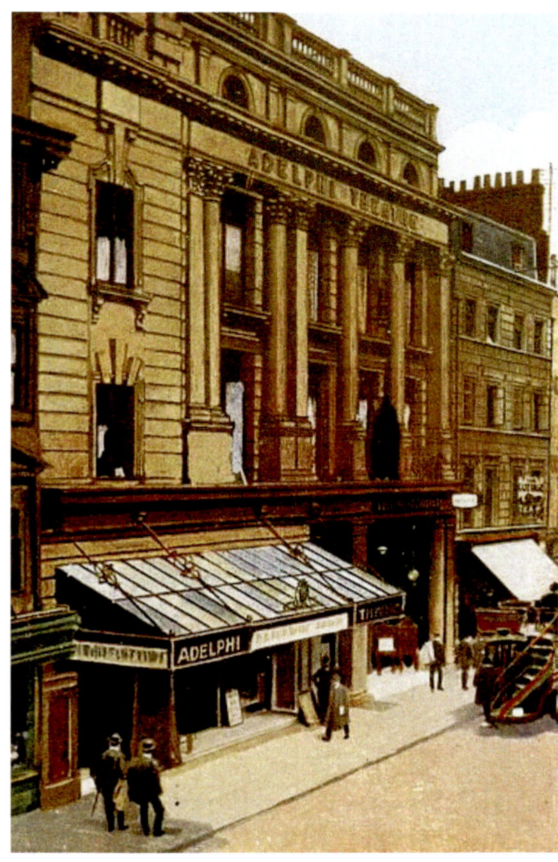

Adelphi Theatre, early 1900s.

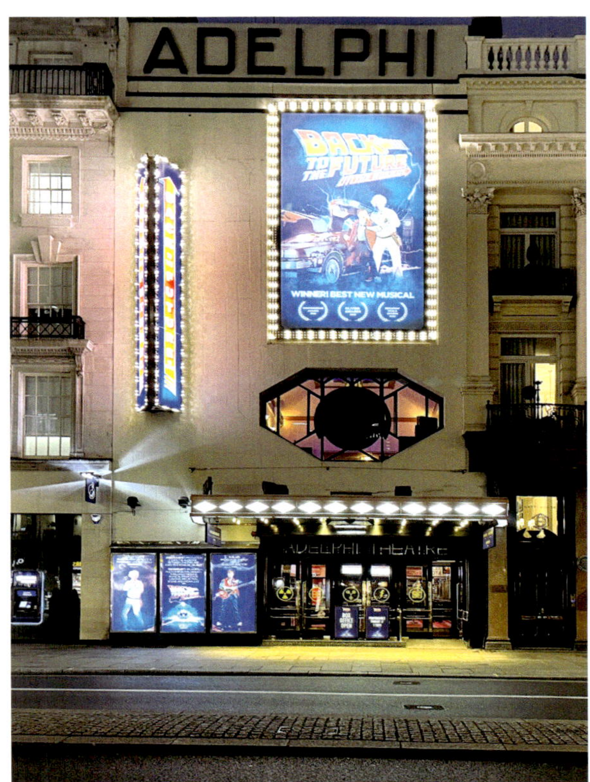

New future: the Adelphi, remodelled in 1930.

Though runs of successful musicals at the Adelphi continue, with recent productions such as *The Bodyguard, Made in Dagenham, Kinky Boots,* and *Back to the Future*, the theatre had previously come under threat of closure in 1968, when the Greater London Council proposed redeveloping Covent Garden, plans affecting several other nearby theatres. After a campaign by actors union Equity, the Musicians' Union, and theatre owners, supported by the theatre-going public, the scheme was eventually abandoned.

One of the other theatres that also came under threat of demolition was the Vaudeville to the north of the Strand, erected in 1926, the third to occupy the site. The first theatre was built between two properties at the front and the Bentinck Club to the rear, opening on 16 April 1870 with a comedy production, *For Love or Money*, by Andrew Halliday. Refurbished and enlarged by owner Thomas Thorne in 1889, reopening with the comedy *Woodbarrow Farm* by Jerome K. Jerome in January 1891, after a succession of productions and theatre managers over the following thirty-five years, the Vaudeville was reconstructed to a design by Robert Adkins, which retained the existing façade but completely reshaped the interior, raising the roof and lowering part of the basement.

Grade II listed in 1972, with a seating capacity of just under 700, Vaudeville productions have not only included musicals and comedies but also popular farces, such as Noel Coward's revival *Present Laughter*, performed during the mid-1970s, *Blithe Spirit*, which ran during the mid-1980s, and more recently Oscar Wilde's final play, *The Importance of Being Ernest*.

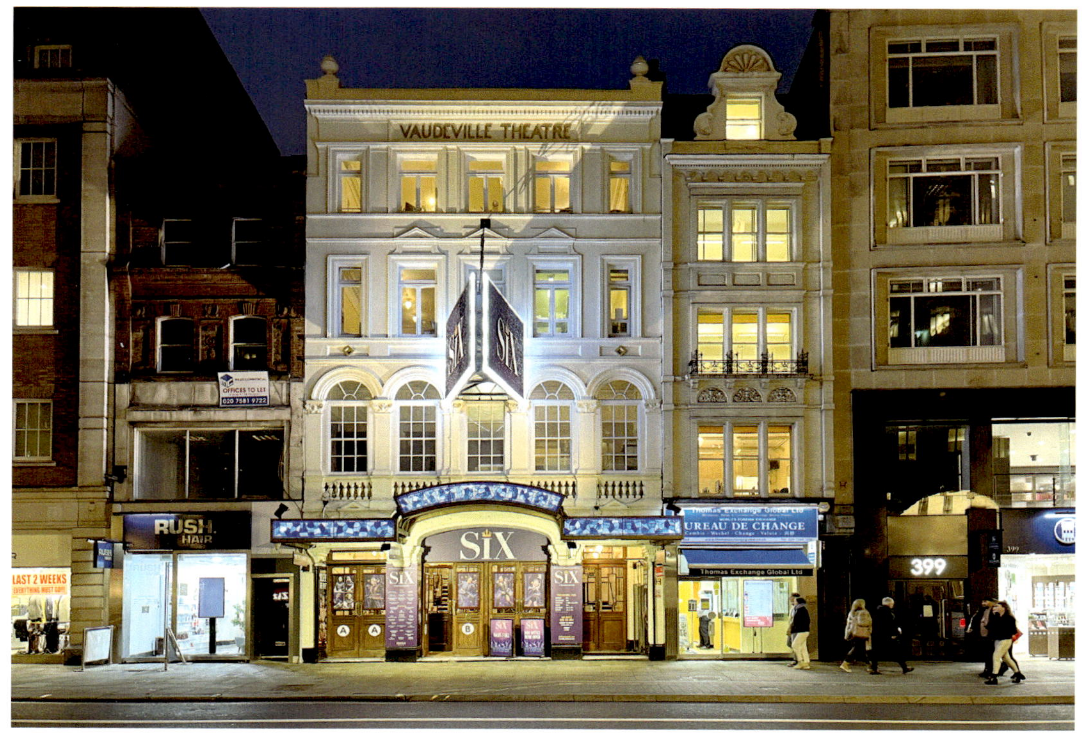

At the Vaudeville Theatre, an all-female cast perform in the musical *Six*, 2023.

Oscar Wilde had written the play while engaged in an ongoing feud with the Marquess of Queensbury, who was intent on revealing Wilde's homosexuality after the author and playwright began having an intimate relationship with the marquess's son Lord Alfred Douglas, as well as liaisons with several other young men whom Wilde entertained at a suite in the Savoy Hotel just off the Strand. Fifteen weeks after the play's premier at St James's Theatre in February 1895, losing the private libel case taken out against Queensbury, Wilde was imprisoned for gross indecency. Considered an intellectual genius and inspirational wit of the age, the poet, playwright, and author spent two years serving hard labour, and when released sailed for France where he died three years later.

Next to the hotel where Wilde conducted his illicit affairs, a new theatre opened with a production of Gilbert and Sullivan's *Patience*, also known as *Bunthorne's Bride*, which premiered in October 1881. The theatre was intended to be named the Beaufort, as the main entrance was located on Beaufort Street, leading to the Embankment; however, the eventual name chosen was the Savoy, both the hotel and theatre erected on the site of the demolished Savoy Palace and Hospital. Rebuilt in the early 1900s, the theatre's exterior was retained but the theatre was completely reconstructed within, and the main entrance moved to the right of The Savoy Hotel's concourse.

Close to the Thames Embankment, south of the Savoy, are two additional theatres, The Playhouse and Charing Cross Theatre. Erected directly adjacent to Charing Cross station, The Playhouse was originally known as the Avenue Theatre, which opened in 1882. The

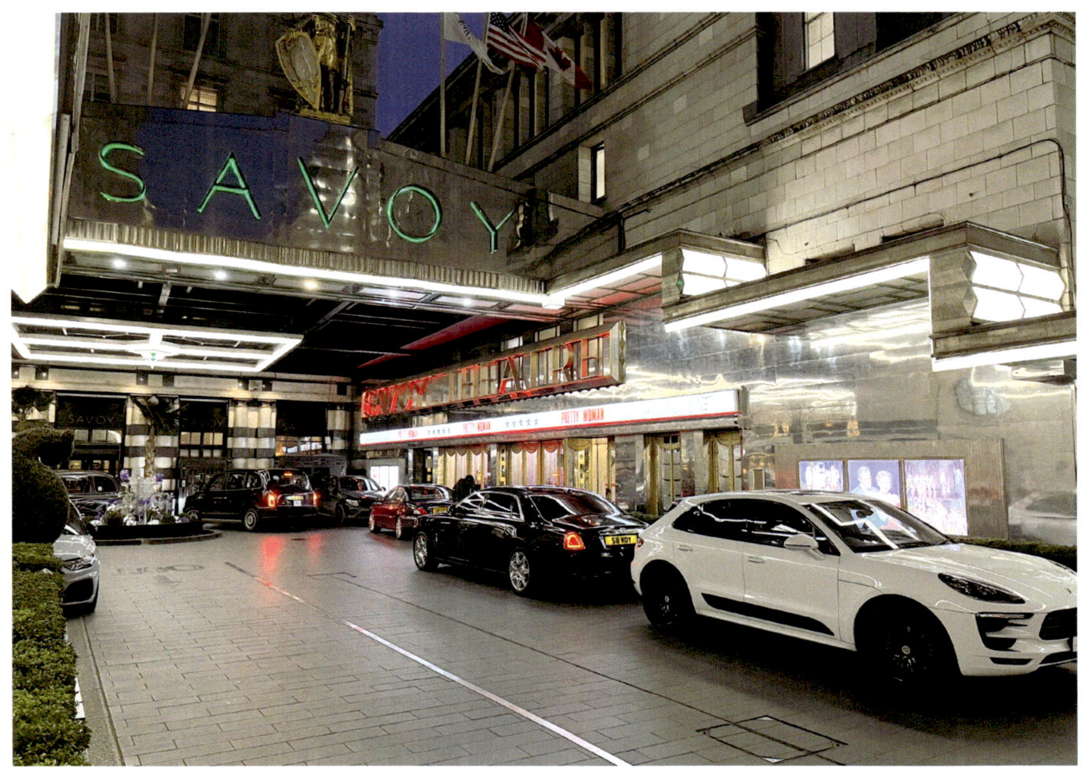

Savoy Theatre, staging *Pretty Woman*, early 2023.

theatre's interior was severely damaged when part of the station collapsed down upon it in 1905, killing six workmen carrying out refurbishments. Reconstructed inside, the exterior was retained after repair. The theatre reopened as The Playhouse in 1907. From 1951, The Playhouse was used by the BBC as a broadcasting studio for twenty-five years, before going dark, a phrase used to describe a theatre without productions, and was left abandoned for ten years before reopening in the 1980s.

The Charing Cross Theatre, situated below the main line station, was originally a pub named The Arches, constructed within the brick-built supporting arches of the station, later converted into Gatti's Charing Cross Music Hall in 1867. Renamed the Players' Theatre, from 1946 to 2002, Victorian-style music hall productions were staged before coming under the management of Broadway producer Steven M. Levy and Sean Sweeny in 2011, the name changing to the Charing Cross Theatre.

Another theatre later converted into a broadcasting studio was the Whitehall Theatre, erected and opened in 1930 on the site of Ye Olde Ship Tavern, to a design by architect E. A. Stone, with the art deco style interior created by Marc-Henri Levy and Gaston Laverdet, who both worked on designing the interiors of several London theatres. The first performance was a play *The Way to Treat a Woman* by American playwright and the theatre's licensee Walter 'Long Run' Hackett, who gained the nickname through the number of his popular plays which ran for over a hundred West End performances.

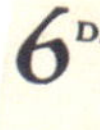

Programme from period true life medical drama *The Human Touch*.

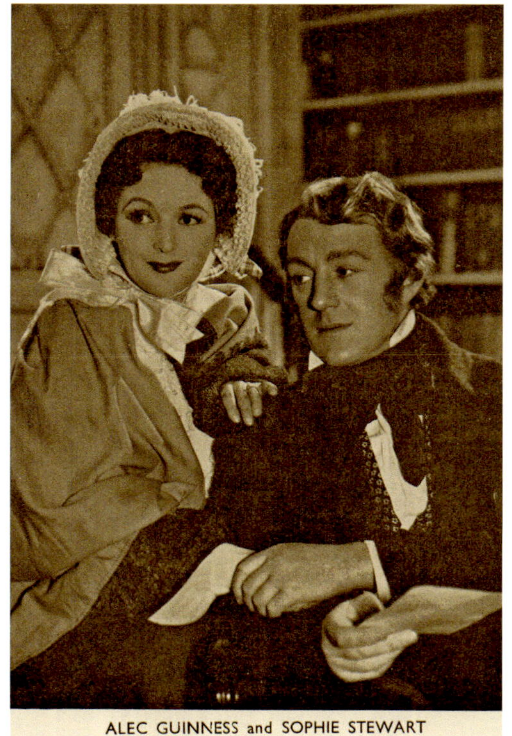

Starring Alec Guinness and Sophie Stewart, *The Human Touch* ran for 113 performances in 1949.

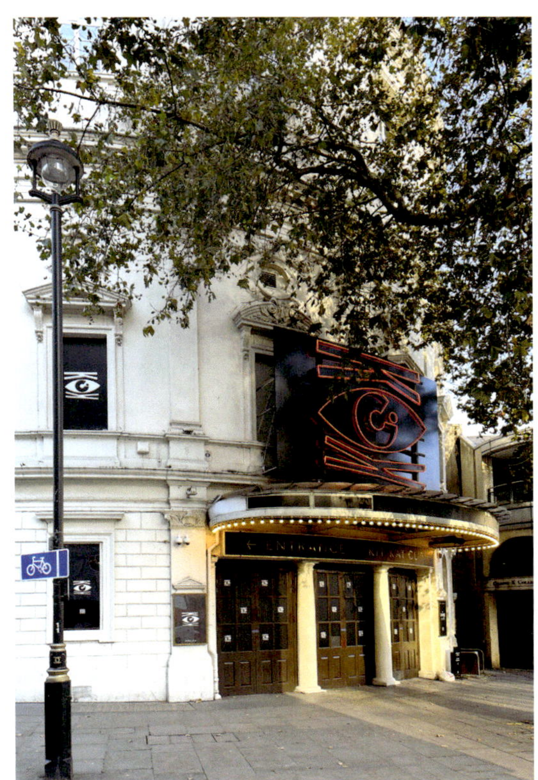

Playhouse, Northumberland Avenue,
transformed into the Kit Club for
Cabaret, 2023.

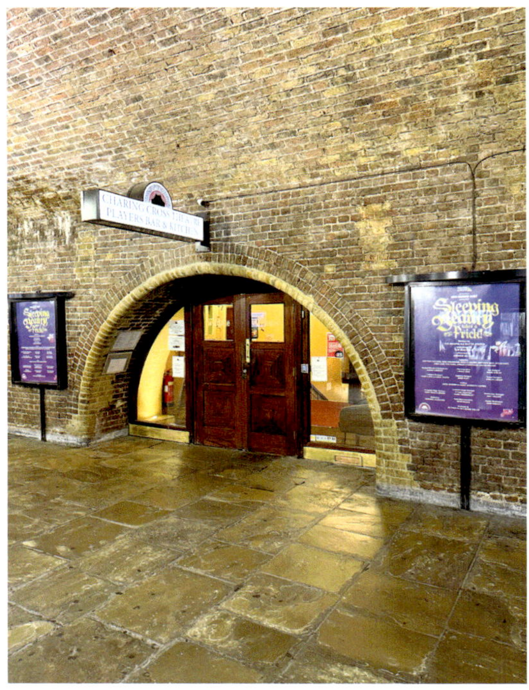

Charing Cross Theatre, The Arches,
Villiers Street.

Presenting mainly reviews, comedies, and farces, manager and actor Brian Rix staged several long-running farces at the Whitehall Theatre during the 1950s and 1960s, and towards the end of the swinging sixties, Paul Raymond, Soho strip club owner and publisher of soft pornography, produced a controversial sex comedy *Pyjama Tops*, which ran for five years. Various productions followed until Whitehall Theatre was converted into a radio and television studio in the late 1900s. Refurbished in 2004, presenting short-run plays and musical revivals, the theatre was completely remodelled inside during 2020 and renamed Trafalgar Theatre.

The area of Soho, where Paul Raymond's strip clubs and sex shops were once located, in previous times, had been a fashionable district of London's aristocracy. However, after an outbreak of cholera in the late nineteenth century, the rich and wealthy residents moved away, replaced by lower class members of society, prostitutes and an assortment of ne're-do-wells. Encompassed by Oxford Street to the north, Charing Cross Road to the east, Regent Street to the west, and at the south Shaftesbury Avenue, Soho became a locality commonly noted for its drinking houses, music halls, and brothels.

Although no longer associated as a place of salacious recreation, theatres built at the turn of the twentieth century, and those coming after, although offering theatregoers a diverse variety of live entertainment, productions were constrained by strict censorship laws.

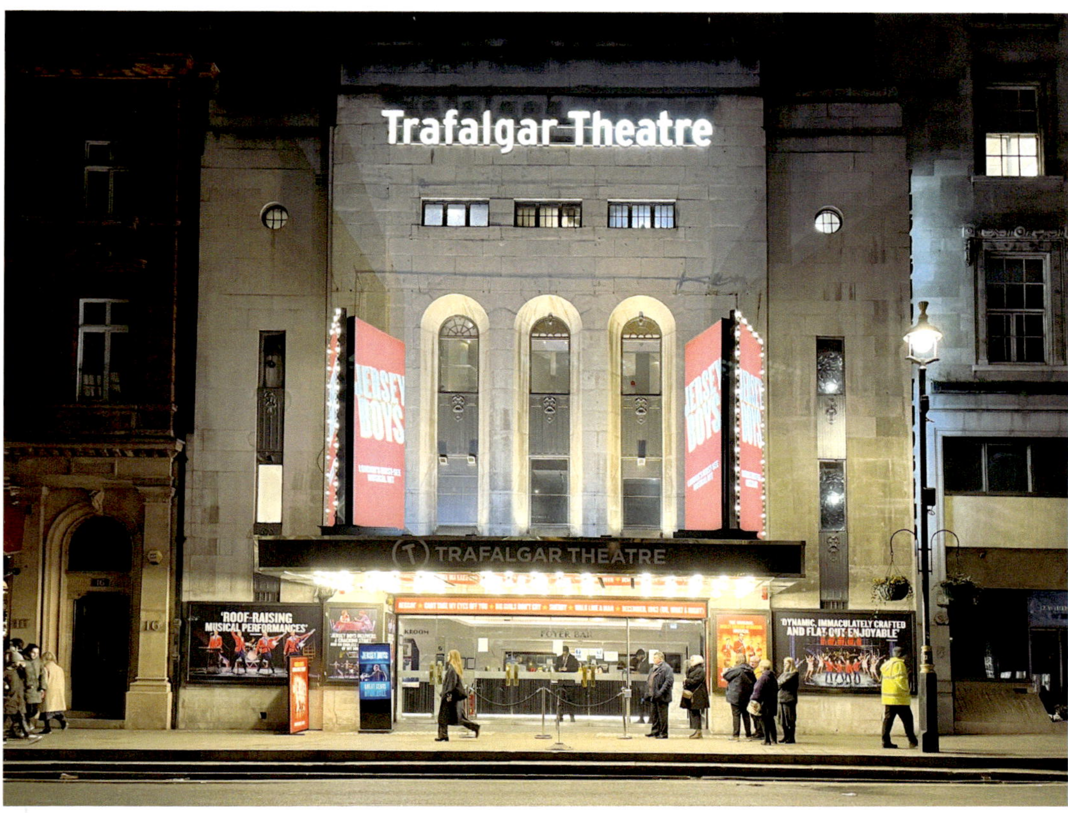

Trafalgar Theatre on Whitehall.

Situated on Great Windmill Street, where a windmill had once stood since at least the mid-1600s, was one of Soho's earliest theatres, the Windmill, which navigated around the censorship laws when glamourous nude women first appeared on stage in 1932.

Originally built for showing silent films in 1909, the Palais de Luxe, as it was then named, was acquired by wealthy widow Laura Henderson, who founded the Windmill Theatre for staging variety productions. Henderson went into partnership with manager Vivian Van Damm, who came up with the idea of Revudeville, a production incorporating singers, dancers, and showgirls, and although at first these productions lost money, things changed with the introduction of naked women in artistic poses, inspired by acts performed at Moulin Rouge, Paris.

Theatrical censor, the Lord Chamberlain, was persuaded acts at the Windmill were not obscene, but live works of art presented in still postures like classic statues. As long as the women did not physically move, although scenery or props were allowed to move, the stationary women on the stage were permitted. Performing throughout the Second World War, Windmill productions became a huge financial success. After Henderson died in 1944, Van Damm inherited the Windmill and continued to stage shows until his own death in 1960. During that time under his management, it was where many young comedians began their careers, such as Peter Sellers, Tony Hancock, Bruce Forsyth, Tommy

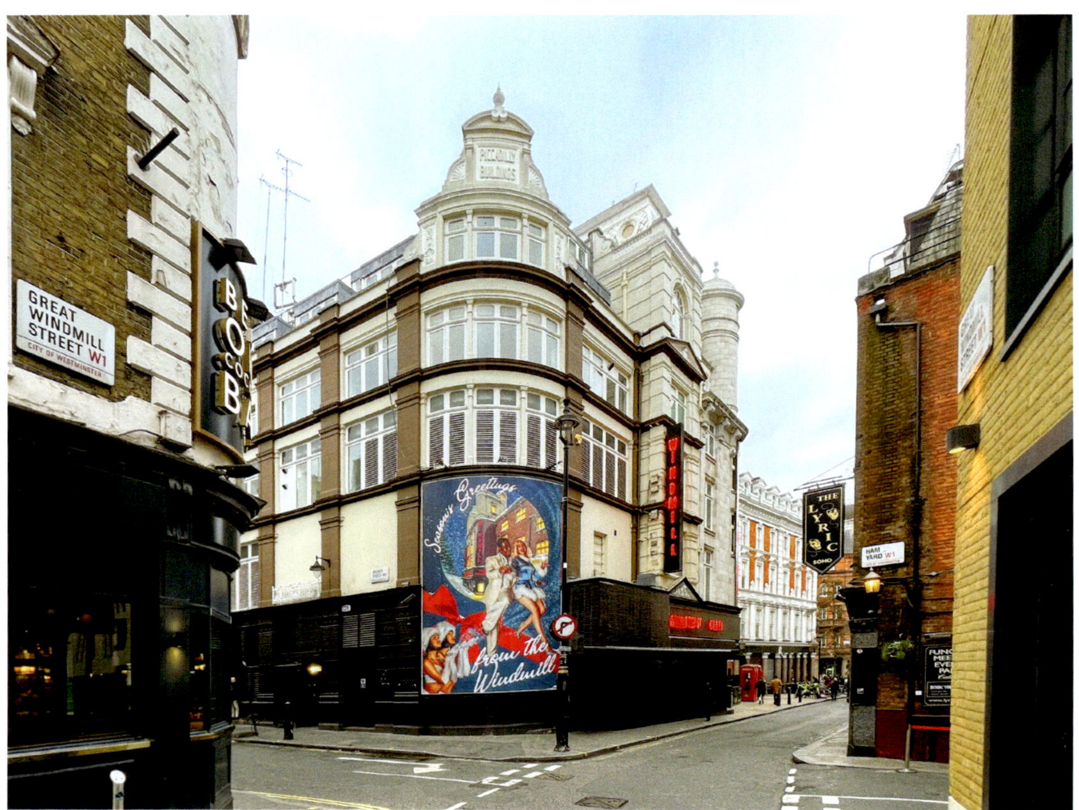

The celebrated Windmill Theatre, Soho.

Cooper, and Harry Secombe. After closing in late 1964, the Windmill was transformed into a cinema, then a nightclub, Paul Raymond's nude revue, a burlesque supper club, and eventually a cabaret and bar.

To the south of Great Windmill Street, towards Piccadilly Circus, between 1885 and 1931, eight theatres opened on Shaftesbury Avenue: London Pavilion, Lyric, Apollo, Hicks, Queen's, Palace, Saville, and Shaftesbury. The first to be built, the London Pavilion, a luxurious and elegant music hall that replaced an older music hall of the same name, opened in November 1885 with a revue starring comedian and music hall artist Arthur Lloyd, accompanied by many popular performers of the day.

After staging a succession of popular musicals, the London Pavilion was converted into a cinema in 1934 and later gutted and rebuilt as a shopping centre with exhibition spaces.

The Lyric, designed by prominent theatre architect Charles Phipps, opened in December 1888 with a comic opera, *Dorothy*. Built for theatre producer Henry Leslie, the Lyric was constructed over four levels with a seating capacity of just over 1,300.

The Lyric's façade was fashioned from red brick and Portland stone in the Renaissance style and is the oldest theatre on Shaftesbury Avenue. Many musical comedies and musicals have been staged at the Lyric, as well as non-musical productions from Shakespeare to Alan Bennet plays.

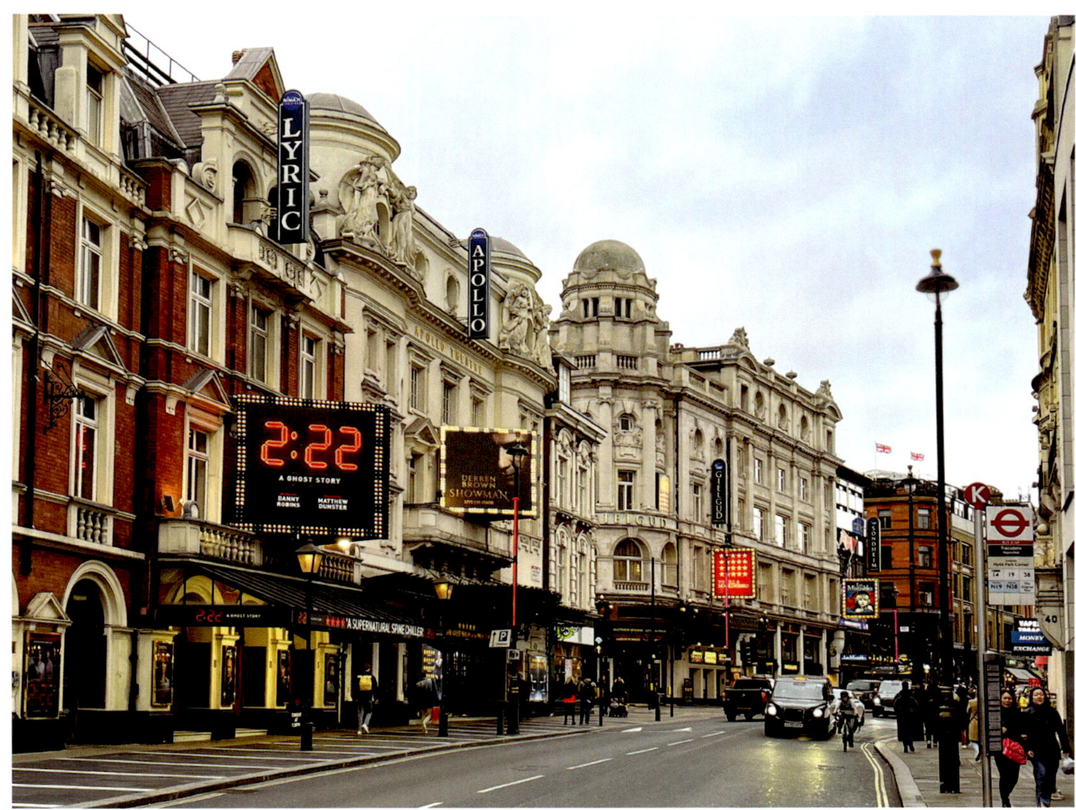

Shaftesbury Avenue theatres. From the left: Lyric, Apollo, Gielgud and Sondheim.

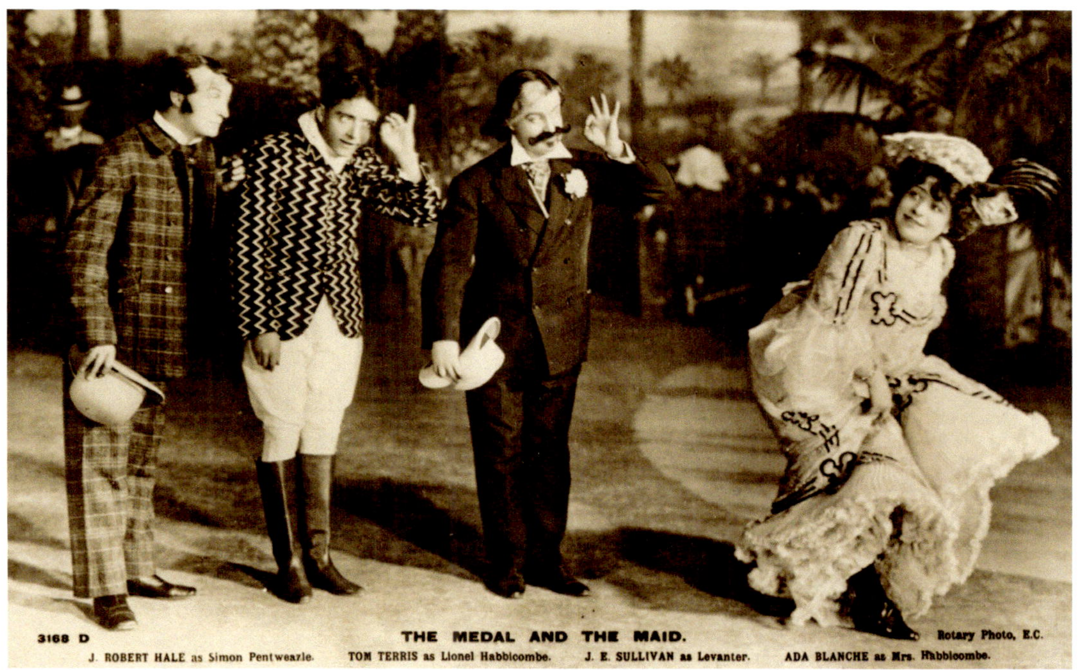

Publicity postcard for the musical comedy *The Medal and the Maid*, which premiered at the Lyric in 1903.

Immediately next door, part of the same block, is the Apollo, originally intended to be named Mascot. Designed by architect Lewin Sharp in a Renaissance style, constructed of stone, brick and steel over four levels, the interior was decorated in the Louis XIV style, with a seating capacity of 1,200. Built for owner Henry Lowenfeld and completed in 1901, the Apollo opened with a private and then public performance of the musical *The Belle of Bohemia*.

Although the American musical was not well received, many future productions ensured the Apollo's ongoing success in staging many classic revival and contemporary musicals.

On the adjacent block, both Hicks and Queen's were built as twin theatres, designed by William Sprague, with frontages constructed of Portland stone. The first to open in 1906 was named after Seymour Hicks, who, along with his writing partner Cosmo Hamilton, owned the theatre. The opening night premiere of the musical play *The Beauty of Bath* was written by Hicks and Hamilton.

Decorated throughout in ivory white and gold, with rose pink upholstery, curtains, and wallpaper, the interior, with a seating capacity over three levels of 1,200, was constructed throughout in fire-resistant material. Renamed the Globe in 1909, the theatre's name changed again when Shakespeare's Globe opened on the Southbank. In recognition of actor Sir John Gielgud, who appeared on stage at the theatre in many successful productions, the theatre was named the Gielgud in 1994.

The Queen's Theatre, named after Queen Alexandra, wife of Edward VII, opened in 1907 with the production *The Sugar Bowl* by Madeleine Lucette Ryley. The theatre was praised

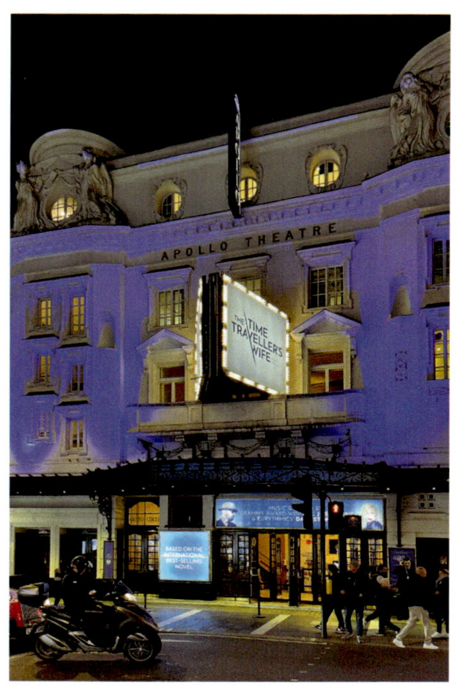

A musical for modern times: a stage adaptation of *The Time Traveller's Wife* at the Apollo.

for its interior decorations of white and gold with green upholstery, curtains, and carpets, if not for the initial performance. In 1940, during the Blitz, a bomb struck the theatre, destroying the front and lobby, and the theatre remained closed for twenty years until rebuilt and reopened in 1959. Playing host to Cameron Mackintosh's musical production *Les Misérables* from 2004 to 2019, the musical previously staged at the Palace Theatre, after being completely refurbished the musical returned five months later to the renamed Sondheim Theatre, after composer and lyricist Stephen Sondheim.

Towards Charing Cross Road at Cambridge Circus stands the Palace Theatre, originally the Royal English Opera House built for theatrical impresario and composer Richard D'Oyly Carte. Designed by Thomas Collcutt, the magnificent façade of the theatre, with a seating capacity of around 1,400, was constructed in red brick with stonework embellishments, the theatre's upper levels supported by steel cantilevers to give a clear view of the stage from tiers constructed of concrete reducing the risk of fire. The theatre opened with Arthur Sullivan's romantic opera *Ivanhoe* in 1891. However, after its run, Carte had no subsequent operatic productions to follow, leasing the theatre to French actress Sarah Bernhardt for a season, after which it was sold and renamed Palace Theatre of Varieties.

Placed somewhere between a music hall and a theatre, regular music hall goers would dress up in their finery travelling into the centre of London's theatreland to be entertained by the top variety acts of the day. When the name changed to the Palace Theatre, a Royal Variety Performance was staged for King George V in 1912. Grade II listed in 1960, productions interchanged between variety acts and musical comedies, and later large-scale productions, including *The Sound of Music, Cabaret, Jesus Christ Superstar, Les Misérables,* and *Harry Potter and the Cursed Child.*

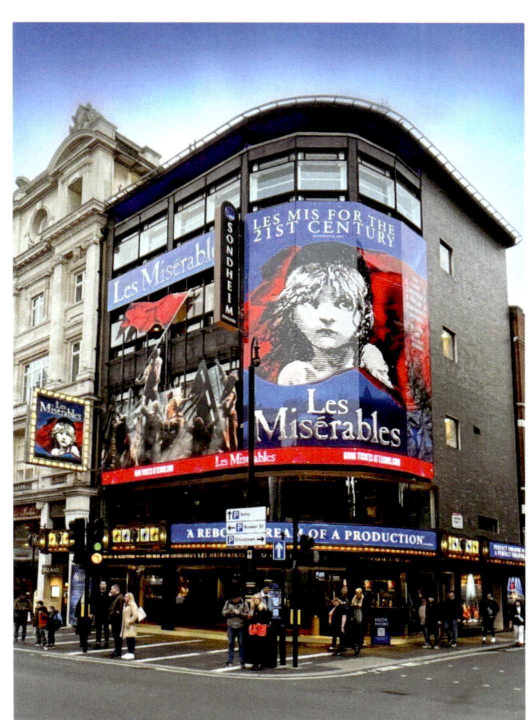

The musical *Les Misérables* staged at the Sondheim.

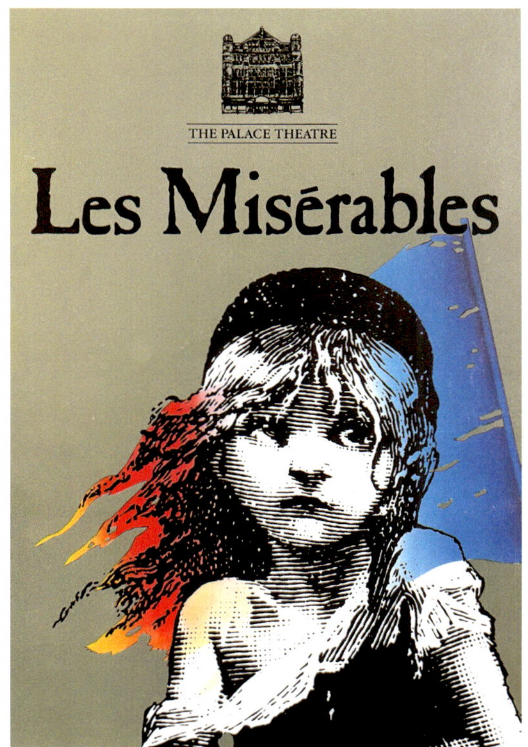

Programme from the Palace Theatre production of *Les Misérables*, with the iconic image of young Cossette taken from an illustration reproduced in the first edition of Victor Hugo's novel which the musical was based upon.

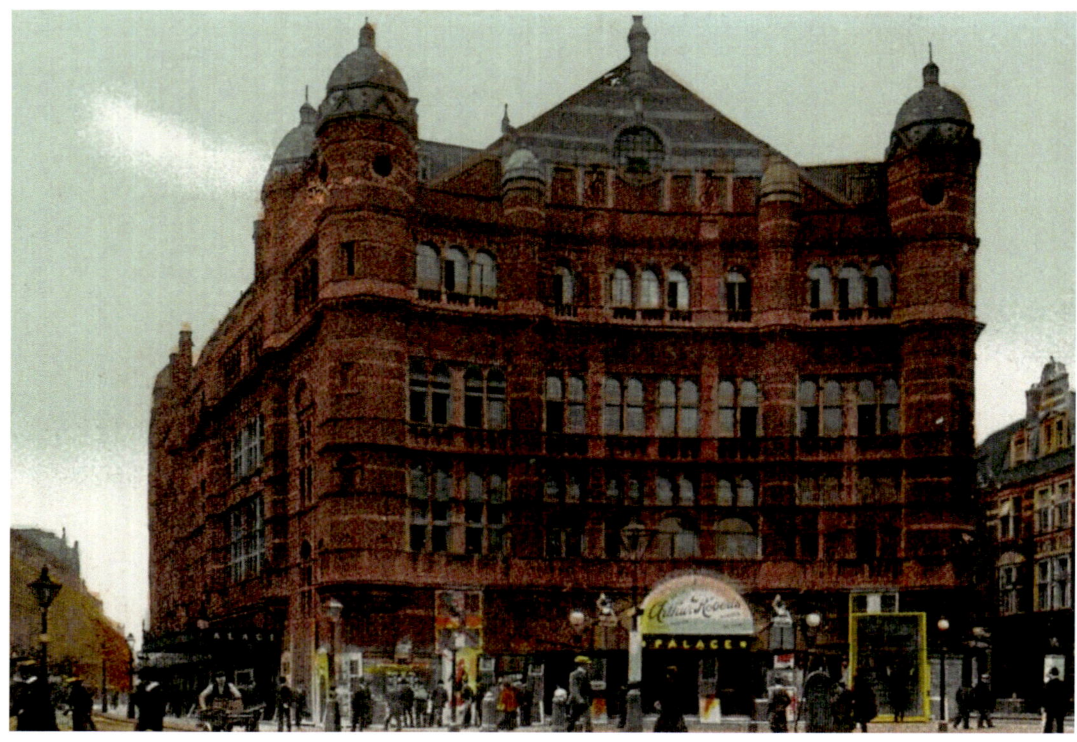

Postcard of the rebuilt Palace Theatre, *c.* 1909.

The first Shaftesbury Theatre, destroyed by bombs in 1941, occupied a site where a fire station stands today, and when first built in 1888 was situated on an isolated plot of land, a period when Shaftesbury Avenue was under development.

The second Shaftesbury Theatre, originally named New Prince's Theatre, was built at the junction of Shaftesbury Avenue and High Holborn in 1911, where most productions were melodramas. With a seating capacity of 2,500, the three-storey steel-framed theatre was faced with terracotta, brick and stone, and topped by a pillared cupola over the main entrance. The theatre was renamed Shaftesbury Theatre after refurbishment in 1963, reopening with the production of Frank Loesser's Broadway musical *How to Succeed In Business Without Really Trying.*

The theatre's new interior décor now had a contemporary feel to it. The house transformed with a new colour scheme of pearl grey with olive reliefs, a magnificent crystal chandelier hanging from the ceiling, and carpets described as similar to those fitted in London's most luxurious hotels. The first production in the UK of the provocative American rock musical *Hair* was first staged at the Shaftesbury in 1968. The show reflected on the 1960s sexual revolution and anti-Vietnam War peace movement. Short of its 2,000th performance, part of the ceiling collapsed, and the theatre temporarily closed. Facing complete demolition in 1973 to make way for a huge road-building programme, a campaign, 'Save London's Theatres', came to the rescue, and along with several other theatres facing closer, the Shaftesbury was saved.

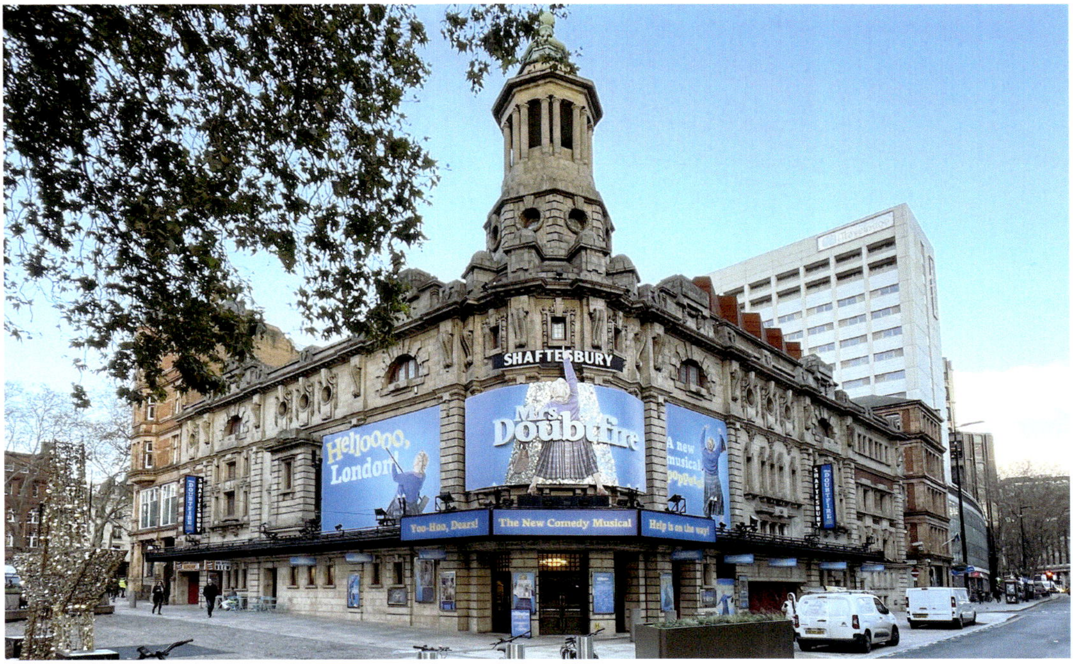

Shaftesbury Theatre, upper Shaftesbury Avenue.

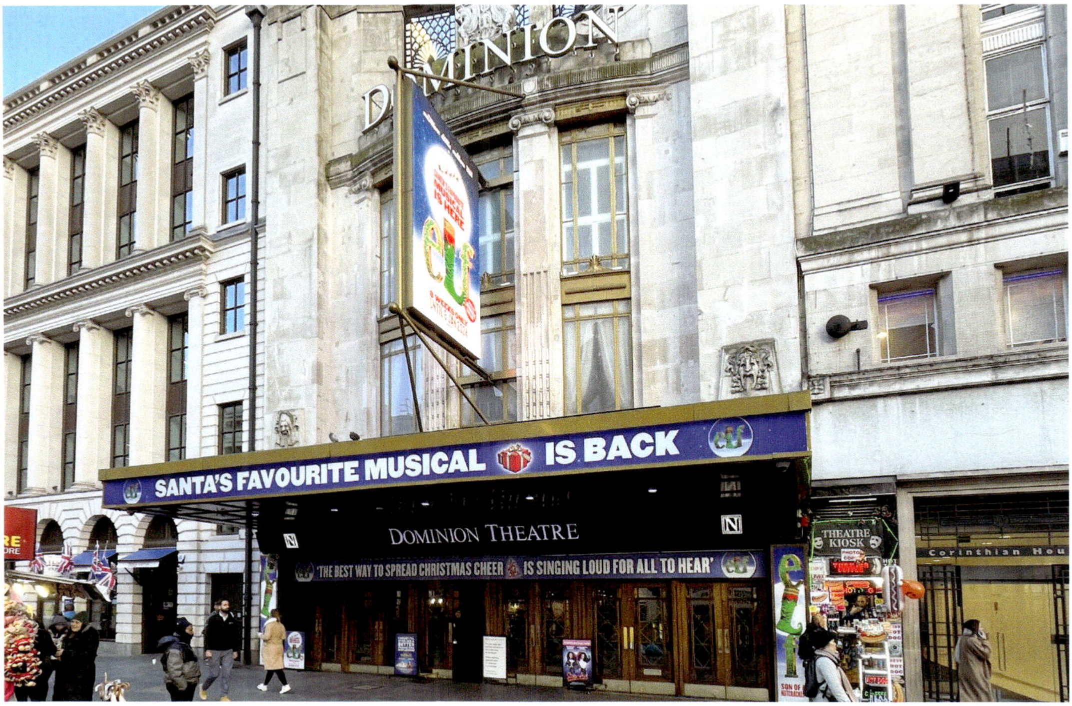

Dominium Theatre, Tottenham Court Road.

On the northern border of Soho, where Oxford Street joins New Oxford Street at Tottenham Court Road, the Dominion Theatre was erected on the site of a former cinema and amusement park, opening in October 1929 with the production *Follow Through*, a two-act golfing musical. The steel-framed theatre with a huge Portland stone front was designed by architects W. & T. R. Milburn, and built by Bovis Ltd for theatre owners Moss Empires.

The house was erected over three levels with a huge capacity of almost 3,000 seats, one of the largest of all London theatres. In the late 1950s, the balcony seats were blocked off when the Dominion was converted into a cinema. Reconverted in the early 1980s to a theatre for large-scale musicals, including *Time*, starring Cliff Richard, and *Barnum*, with Paul Nicholas in the lead role, an extensive restoration and several refurbishments took place between 2014 and 2019.

To the east of the Soho district, on the north of Charing Cross Road, is London's latest theatre, Sohoplace, the first purpose-built West End theatre to open in fifty years. Operated by Nimax Theatres, Sohoplace opened in late 2022, with the dramatic production *Marvellous*, the true life story of Stoke City fan Neil Baldwin. The glamorous high glass-fronted building, designed by architects AHMM, was erected on a neglected corner of Soho, adjacent to the celebrated music venue the London Astoria, demolished to build Crossrail.

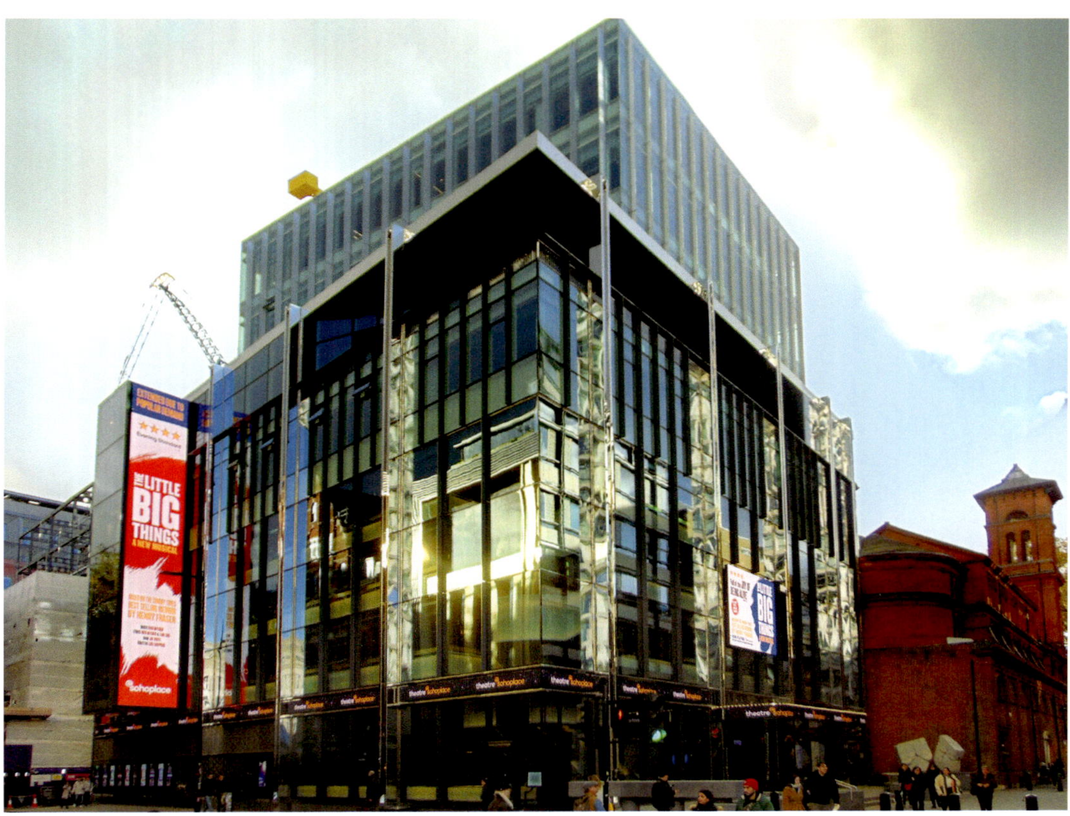

West End's newest theatre, Sohoplace.

With a seating capacity of 602 in the round two-tier auditorium, the stage positioned centrally, the theatre includes an actors' rehearsal room and green room, and restaurant, bar, and terrace.

At the opposite end of Oxford Street, on Argyle Street, is the world-famous London Palladium, home to Royal Variety Performances, Christmas pantomimes, and television production *Sunday Night at the London Palladium*. Created by Jack Parnell, *Sunday Night at the London Palladium* was first hosted by comedian Tommy Trinder, followed by all-round entertainer Bruce Forsyth. After Forsyth died in 2017, his ashes were laid below the theatre's stage and a blue plaque commemorating the popular star was erected on a nearby wall.

Built in 1910 on the site of a former circus, later converted for ice skating, The London Palladium was designed by Frank Matcham for a syndicate headed by theatre proprietor Walter Gibbons. The theatre's house comprised of three levels with a massive seating capacity of 3,435. The interior, decorated in white and gold with rose pink seat upholstery, curtains, and carpets, was described as the last word in luxury. To the rear of the stalls, a ladies' orchestra played in the large Palm Court, where theatregoers would take tea between performances. Hosting a variety of theatrical productions and concerts, in the late 1970s, the Palladium became home to large-scale musicals, including a revival of *The King and I*,

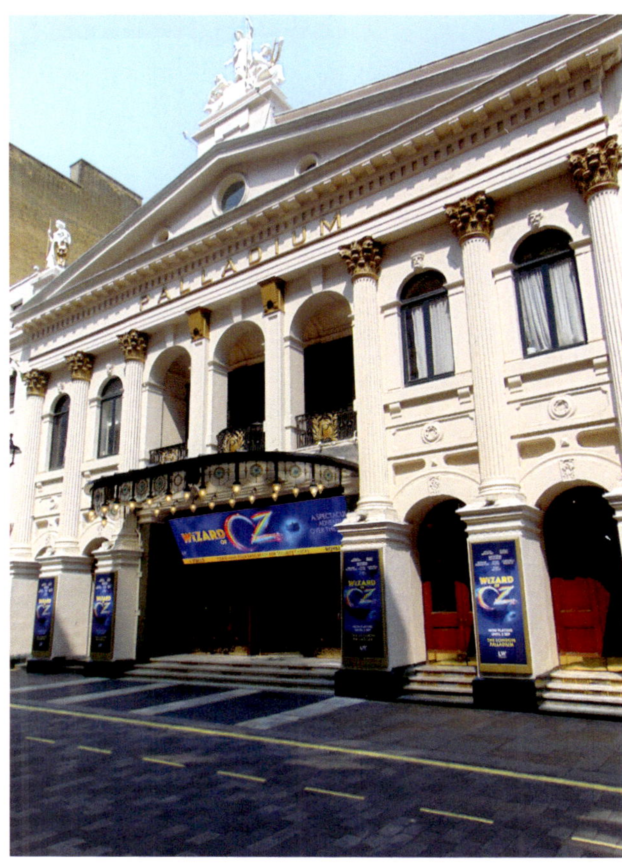

London Palladium, Argyll Street.

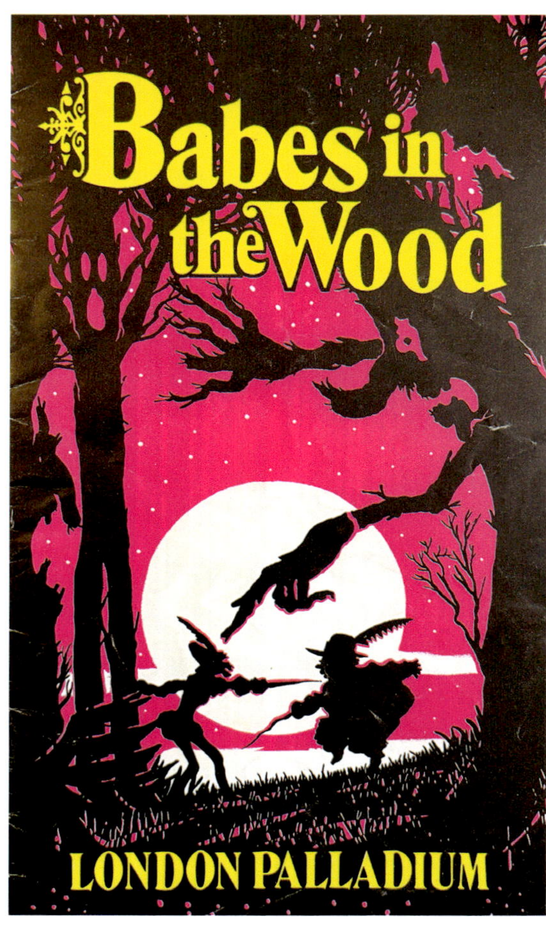

Programme from the 1972 production of *Babes in the Woods* starring Edward Woodward and Adrienne Posta.

starring Hollywood legend Yul Brynner and British star Virginia McKenna. The Palladium was also well known for staging annual Christmas pantomimes, which began post-Second World War, including classics such as *Cinderella, Puss in Boots, Dick Whittington, Mother Goose, Aladdin, Babes in the Woods,* and *Jack and the Beanstalk.*

In the far south-west corner of Soho, tucked away on Denman Street, is the Piccadilly Theatre, built in 1928 to the design of architects Bertie Crowe and Edward Stone for impresario Edward Laurillard. Constructed in steel and concrete, the art deco-style interior was decorated throughout in cream, shades of green, and gold, with a seating capacity of just over 1,400. The opening production, *Blue Eyes*, a historical musical romance was set during the Jacobite rising, starred leading lady Evelyn Laye, playing an actress disguised as a soldier.

Staging a variety of productions, the theatre was briefly converted into a cinema before the Second World War and was another London theatre damaged during hostilities when it was hit by a flying bomb. After repair, the Piccadilly staged many classical plays by Shakespeare and Marlowe, along with contemporary productions by Tom Stoppard, Willy Russell, and Samuel Beckett.

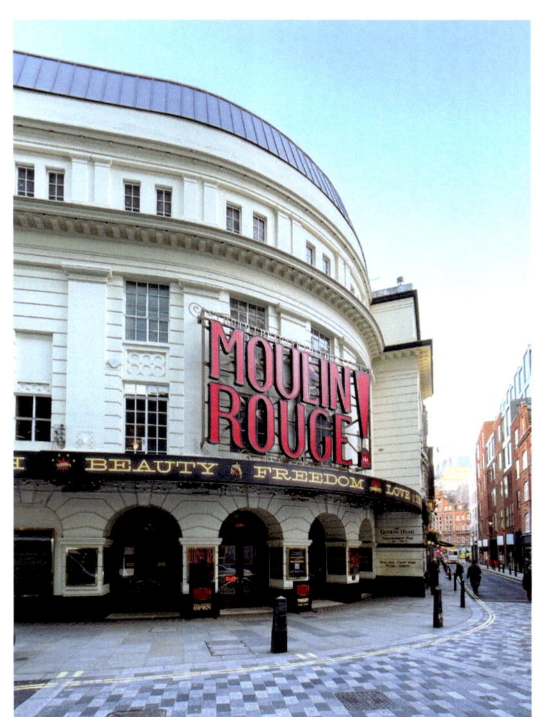

Piccadilly Theatre, Denman Street.

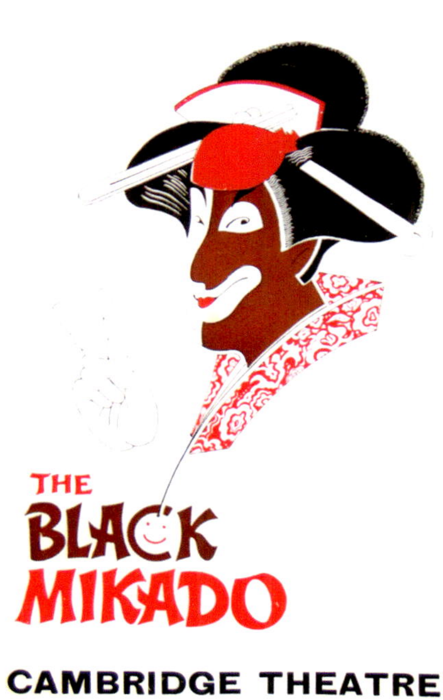

Programme from *The Black Mikado*
premier, the Cambridge Theatre, 1975.

The Piccadilly's opening was followed by the building of several more London theatres during 1930. the Prince Edward on Old Compton Street, named after the then Prince of Wales, was the first, opening with a performance of *Rio Rita*, a musical comedy. Designed by Edward Stone in the character of an Italian palace, the interior over three levels was art deco in style, furnished in rose pink and purple. Under various managers, the theatre has intermittently been a cinema and cabaret, known as The London Casino. Like many London theatres, the Prince Edward closed at the outbreak of the Second World War and was then used for a period as a services club, before reopening with a series of classical plays, dramas, romantic comedies, and musicals.

The second to open in 1930, at Seven Dials, was the Cambridge Theatre, which premiered with a review, *Charlotte's Masquerade*. The theatre reflected a modernist German-style exterior, constructed of steel and concrete, designed by architects Wimperis, Simpson and Guthrie. The house had a capacity of 1,275 over three levels. The Cambridge became home to several successful new plays and revivals and in 1975, the theatre staged the premiere of *The Black Mikado*, an adaptation of Gilbert and Sullivan's comic opera with an all but one black cast. After refurbishment in the late 1980s, the Cambridge hosted seasonal pantomimes and a succession of topical musicals.

In September 1930, the Phoenix rose from the ashes, or rubble, of a former music hall, the Alcazar, which once occupied the site. Built for Sydney Bernstein, later Lord Bernstein,

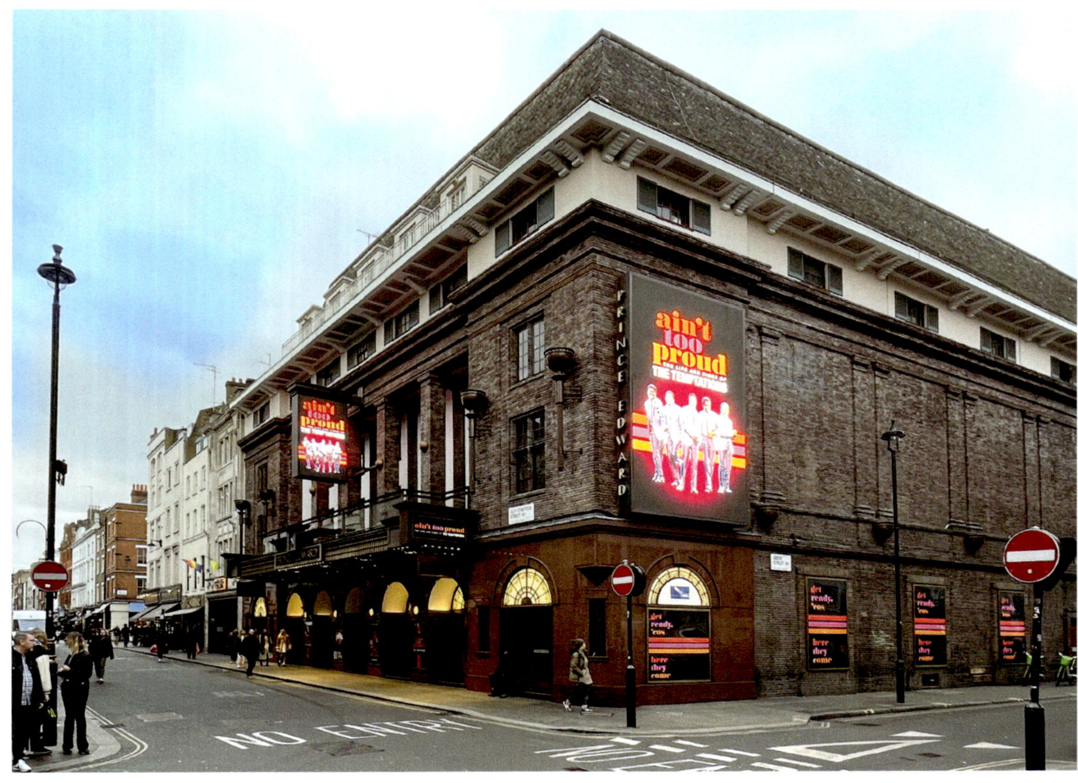

Prince Edward Theatre, Old Compton Street.

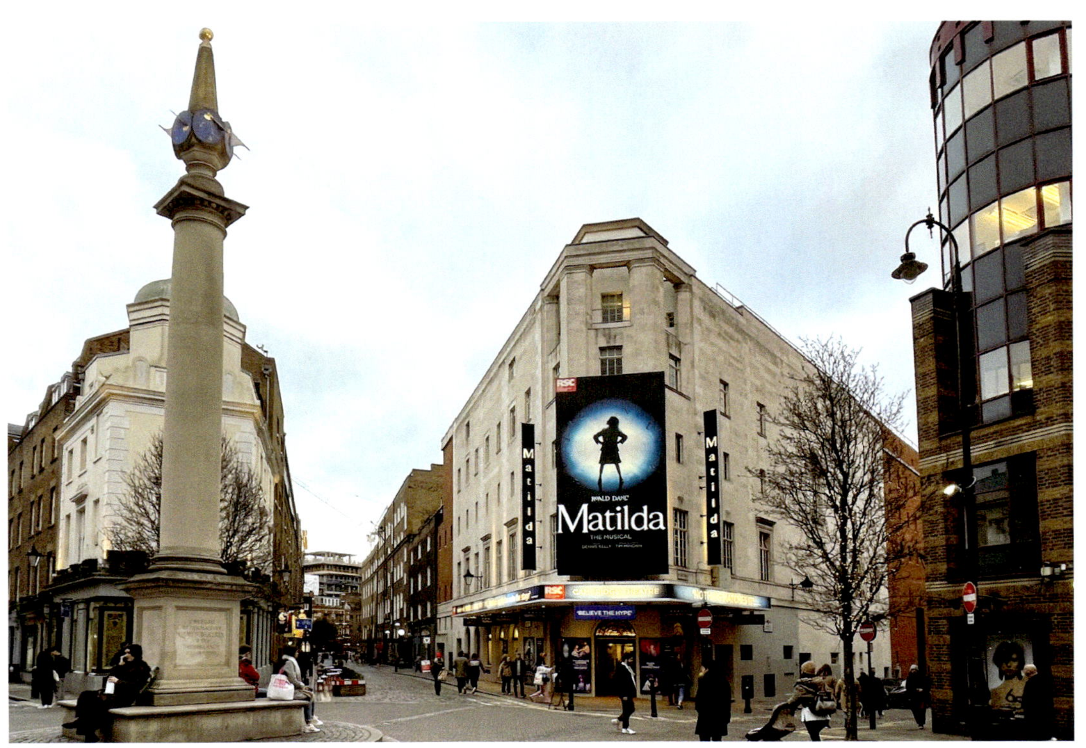

Cambridge Theatre, Earlham Street, Seven Dials.

to a design by architects Sir Giles Gilbert and Bertie Crewe, the theatre's exterior was neoclassical with an Italianate-style interior. The Phoenix opened with Noël Coward's *Private Lives*, starring the author, alongside Gertrude Lawrence and a young Laurance Olivier in his first theatrical success. In the early 1950s, Shakespeare's *The Winter's Tale* was staged starring John Gielgud, then in the late 1960s, a musical adaption of Chaucer's *Canterbury Tales* ran for around 2,000 performances. From then onwards the Phoenix has staged various musicals and in 1983, its first pantomime, *Snow White and the Seven Dwarfs*, starring Eurovision Song Contest winner Dana.

The last to be built in 1930 was Leicester Square Theatre, which intended to host live performances and light musical comedy, but on completion, the theatre became home to both live shows and cinematic films. Converted to show only films, Leicester Square Theatre eventually closed and, despite objections, was demolished to make way for a hotel that incorporated a two-screen cinema.

The theatres located around the areas of Leicester Square and adjacent Piccadilly Circus make up a considerable proportion of London's theatreland, from lower Charing Cross Road west toward Regent Street. At the foot of Charing Cross Road, opposite the statue of Henry Irving, is the Garrick Theatre, named after David Garrick. Designed by Walter Emden and Charles Phipps, the building of the Garrick was financed by William Gilbert, successful playwright and writing partner of Arthur Sullivan, who together collaborated on creating fourteen comic operas.

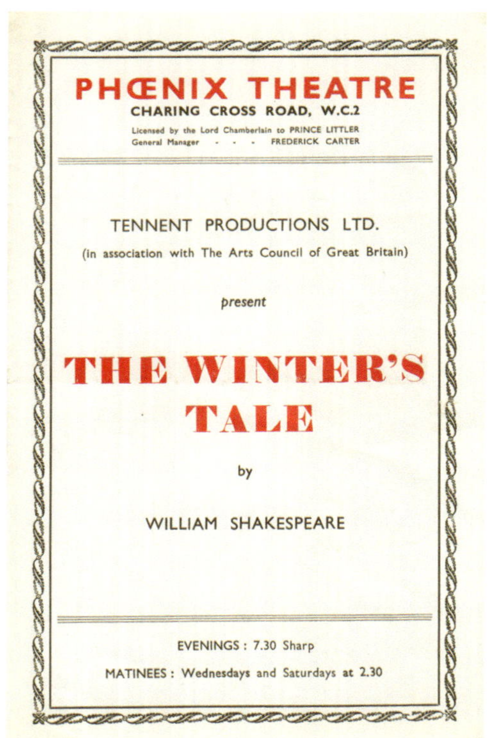

Programme from revival of Shakespeare's *The Winter's Tale*, performed in the summer of 1951.

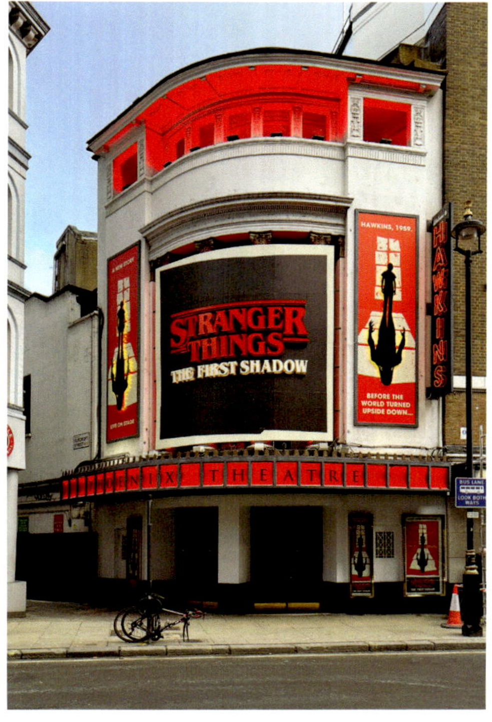

Phoenix, Charing Cross Road.

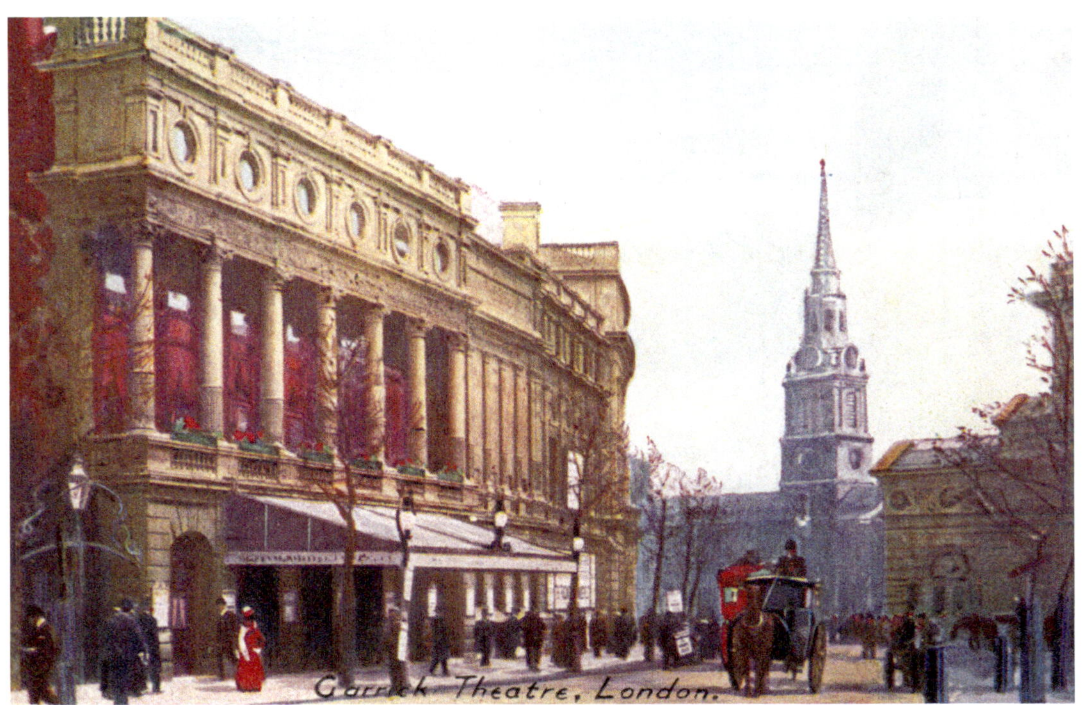

View of the Garrick towards St Martin-in-the-Fields, early 1900s.

The deep excavations carried out to allow the back of the dress circle to be at ground level held up the theatre's construction when an ancient river was discovered running under the site, and there was concern the project may have to be abandoned. Eventually completed in 1889, under the management of actor and manager John Hare, the Garrick opened with the production *The Profligate,* by Arthur Wing Pinero, the first of several plays depicting women's battle against their perceived role in society, the productions creating strong parts for female actors.

The front of the theatre's classical-style façade constructed of Bath and Portland stone stretched 140 feet along the lower east side of Charing Cross Road, the house consisting of four tiers with a seating capacity of 1,300. The interior was decorated in the Italian Renaissance style, the floor of the vestibule laid with mosaic and the furnishings consisting of cherry-red wall hangings around the stalls and dress circle, with the pit walls, upper circle and rest of the interior hung with cherry-red and gold Japanese paper.

Associated with plays, comedies, comedy dramas, and in the 1980s farces, the theatre was acquired by the Stoll Moss Group and then Andrew Lloyd Webber's Really Useful Company and Bridgepoint Capital, before purchased by Nimax Theatres.

A short stroll up Charing Cross Road is Wyndham's Theatre, designed by prominent architect W. G. R. Sprague for actor and theatre proprietor Charles Wyndham, who named the theatre after himself. The theatre opened with the play *David Garrick,* by Thomas Robertson, with Wyndham playing the title role and his future wife, actress Mary Moore, playing Ada Ingot, a young woman with a crush on Garrick. The theatre's house was

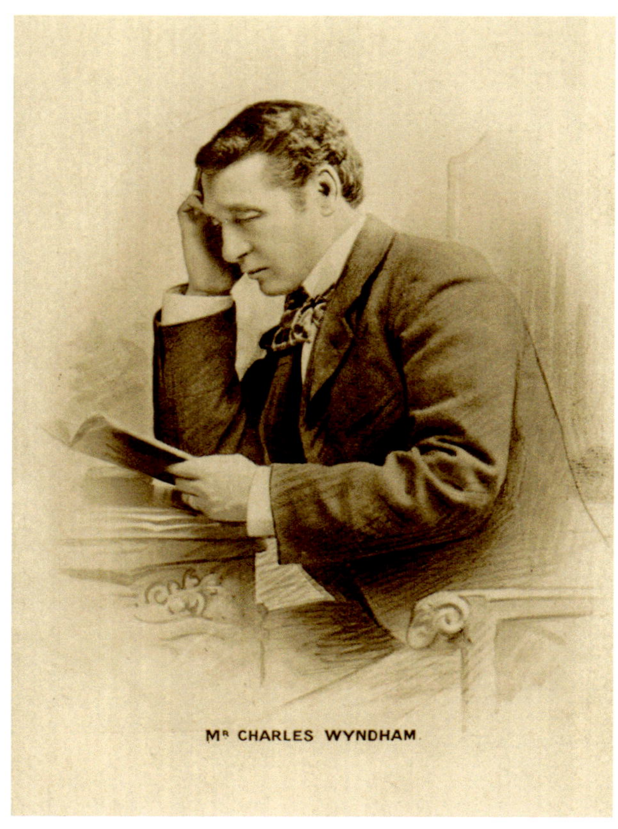

Actor and theatre proprietor
Charles Wyndham.

constructed over three levels, decorated in the style of Louis XVI, with colours of cream
and turquoise blue, and gold gilding. The theatre, at the time it was built, stood in isolation,
described as faced with Portland stone on all sides in the Modern Renaissance style. With
a seating capacity of 759, the theatre was later refurbished to include an extra tier.

A regular performer at Wyndham's since 1910 was actor and manager Gerald du
Maurier, whose young daughter, Daphne, went on to write several novels, biographies, and
plays, including *The Years Between*, which premiered at the theatre in 1945. The romantic
drama, set during the Second World War, became a long-running West End success. In
1953, novelist Graham Green's first play, *The Living Room*, a two-act play that takes place
in one room throughout the production, premiered at Wyndham's, and another first came
in 2002 when music star Madonna made her West End debut in *Up for Grabs*, the play
focussing on finances in the world of art.

After Wyndham completed the construction of his theatre on land that he owned, a large
area was left vacant, and, unable to sell it, he decided to build another theatre named the
New Theatre, after the street opposite, New Row. Once again Wyndham engaged architect
Sprague to design the theatre, which, like Wyndham's, was clad in Portland stone, but
had a larger house with a seating capacity of 877 over four levels. The interior, described
as Free Classical style, was decorated throughout in cream and gold, with Rose Du Barry
upholstery, hangings and curtains.

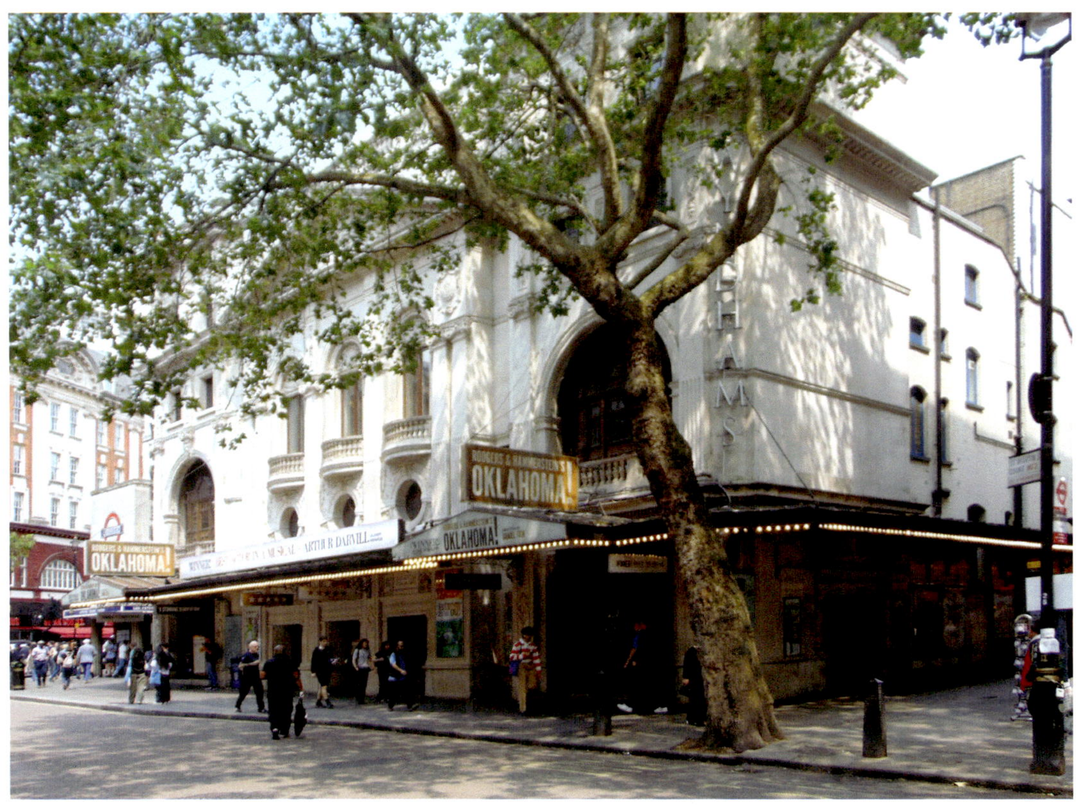

Wyndham Theatre, Charing Cross Road.

The New Theatre opened in March 1903 with the comedy production *Rosemary*, by Louis Parker, both Wyndham and his wife playing the leading characters. Many of the West End's most successful plays were staged at the New Theatre, as well as Noël Coward's first play, *I'll Leave It To You*, which premiered in 1920, and where young actors John Gielgud, Michael Redgrave, Ralph Richardson, Laurance Olivier and Edith Evans performed in several Shakespeare productions. The theatre's name was changed in 1973 to the Albery, in recognition of theatre director Sir Bronson Albrey, and when acquired by Delfont Mackintosh Theatres, the name was changed to the Noël Coward Theatre.

An existing building on the corner of Charing Cross Road and Cranbourn Street, the London Hippodrome, designed by Frank Matcham for Moss Enterprises, opened in 1900 as a music hall and circus with a built-in water tank for spectacular water shows, the first ever seen in London. Completely refurbished twelve years later, with a seating capacity of 1,340, the Hippodrome staged variety productions, reviews, dances, and musical comedies. When impresario Bernard Delfont acquired the theatre in 1958, the interior was reconstructed and converted into a nightclub, The Talk of the Town. Artists appearing included stars Judy Garland, Frank Sinatra, Sammy Davis Junior, Tom Jones, Cliff Richard, and Stevie Wonder. Owned for a time by nightclub owner Peter Stringfellow, in 2012 the theatre was extensively restored to become The London Hippodrome Casino.

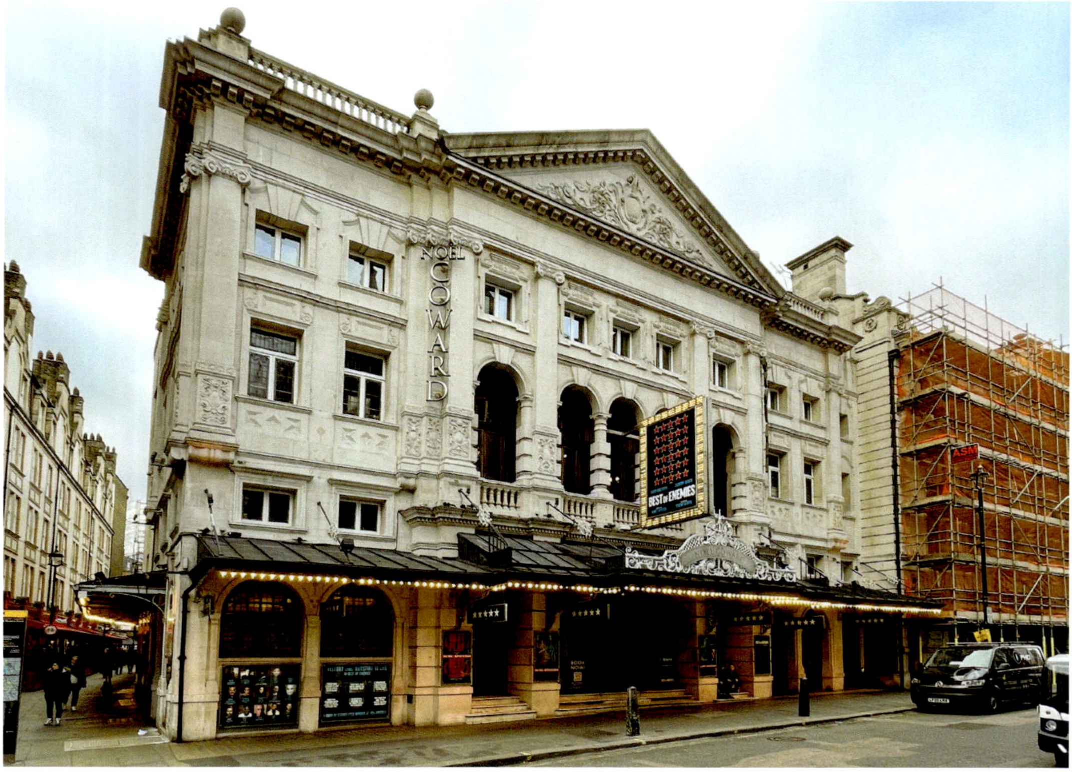

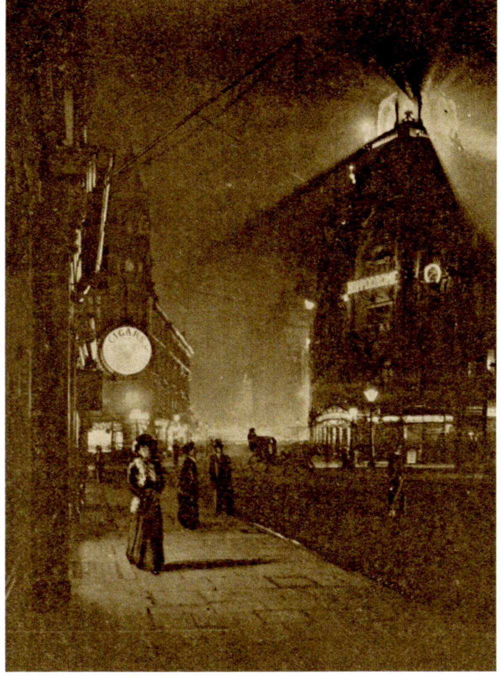

Above: Noel Coward Theatre,
St Martin's Lane.

Left: Hippodrome Circus and Music Hall,
early 1900s.

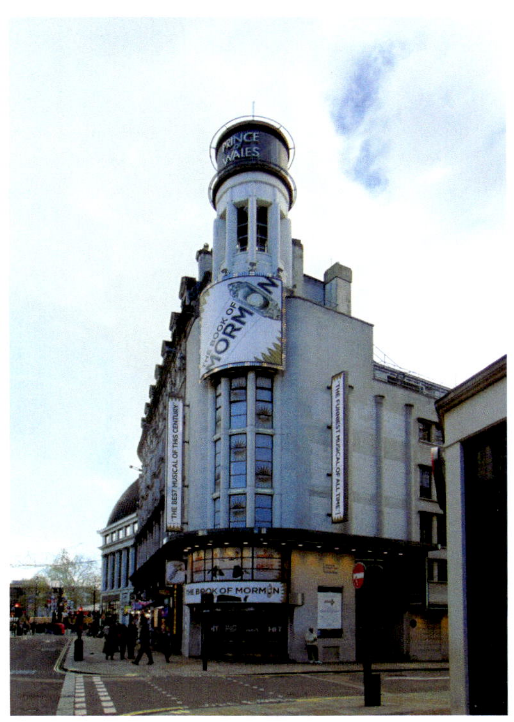

Prince of Wales Theatre, Leicester Square.

To the west of Leicester Square the Prince of Wales Theatre, which opened in 1937, is the second theatre to occupy the site. The first was built in 1884, originally named the Prince's Theatre, and was where Lillie Langtry performed in *Princess George* and *School for Scandal*. Renamed the Prince of Wales Theatre two years after opening, in recognition of the future king, Edward VII, in the early 1930s the theatre staged a series of bawdy follies, which became so successful the profits went towards funding the building of a larger and improved theatre. The original theatre was demolished in June 1937, and a new theatre of the same name erected in its place, the foundation stone laid by music hall star, actress, singer and comedian Gracie Fields, who entertained site workers by belting out a ballad.

Designed by Robert Cromie in the art deco style, the theatre had a bigger stage than the first, as well as a larger house with a capacity of around 1,100. Opening in October 1937, productions continued with a succession of follies, followed by musical comedies and variety shows, and in 1963, The Beatles performed during a Royal Variety Show in the presence of Elizabeth, the Queen Mother. Refurbished in 2004 to increase the seating capacity, the theatre hosted musicals, which began with *Mamma Mia!*, a romantic musical created from a compilation of ABBA songs.

Under a large block of elegant Portland stone-clad buildings facing Piccadilly Circus is The Criterion Theatre, built in 1873, almost entirely below street level. Designed by Thomas Verity, the architect fitted the theatre snuggly below a group of buildings erected the year before on the site of the White Bear Inn. The house, built on three levels, had a seating capacity of 675 and was decorated throughout in light blue, white and gold. The theatre opened in 1874 with a comedy, *An American Lady*, by Henry Byron, along with a one-act

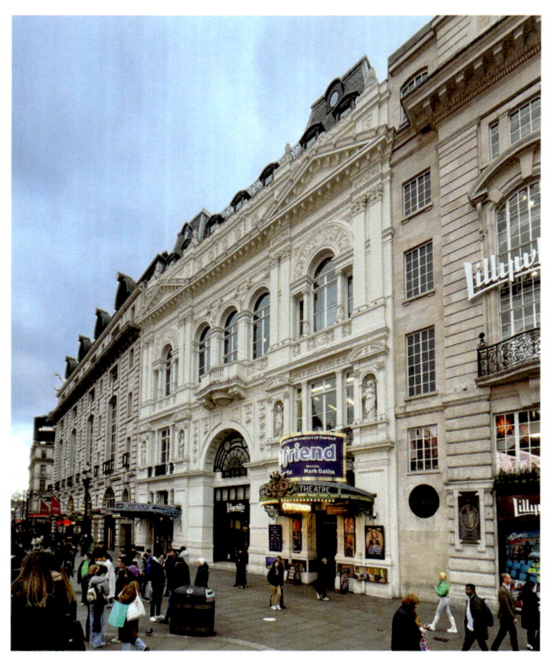

Criterion Theatre, Piccadilly.

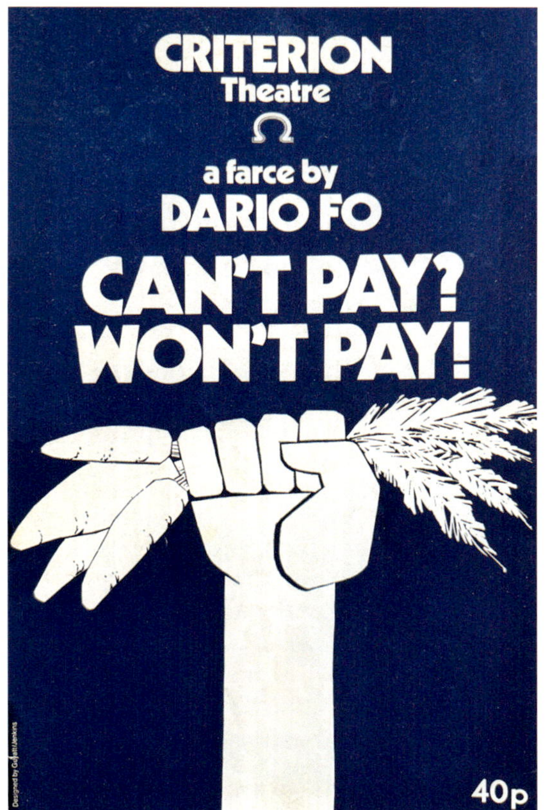

Programme from topical farce *Can't Pay? Won't Pay!*, the first play written by Italian actor and playwright Dario Fo. A production staged at the Criterion in the early 1980s, the cast included Alfred Molina, Maggie Steed and Sylvester McCoy.

musical by William Gilbert and Alfred Cellier. Closed down by the Metropolitan Board of Works because of ventilation concerns, The Criterion was reconstructed internally, which included the installation of electricity, and reopened in 1884. Requisitioned for the BBC during the Second World War, The Criterion was used as an underground broadcasting studio safe from the Blitz. Staging a variety of productions including dramas, musicals, comedies, and farces, The Criterion was renovated between 1989 and 1992.

Another theatre designed by Thomas Verity, The Royal Comedy Theatre off the Haymarket opened in 1881 with an English adaptation, *The Mascotte*, by Edmond Audran, Alfred Duru, and Henri Chivot, the story of a farm girl with mystic powers. The theatre's exterior was built in a classical style with painted stucco and brickwork. The house, over four levels with a seating capacity of 1,186, was decorated in the Renaissance style in white and gold, accompanied by maroon drapery.

Under a series of managers, the theatre staged comic operas, musical comedies, and farces, and in 1956, the New Watergate Club was established at the theatre to overcome censorship laws by staging banned plays under club prerequisites. The plays of actor, playwright, and producer Harold Pinter were often staged at the Comedy Theatre, all having very successful runs, Pinter directing a dramatic production of Simon Gray's *The Old Masters* in 2004. After Pinter's death, the theatre was renamed The Harold Pinter Theatre in his honour.

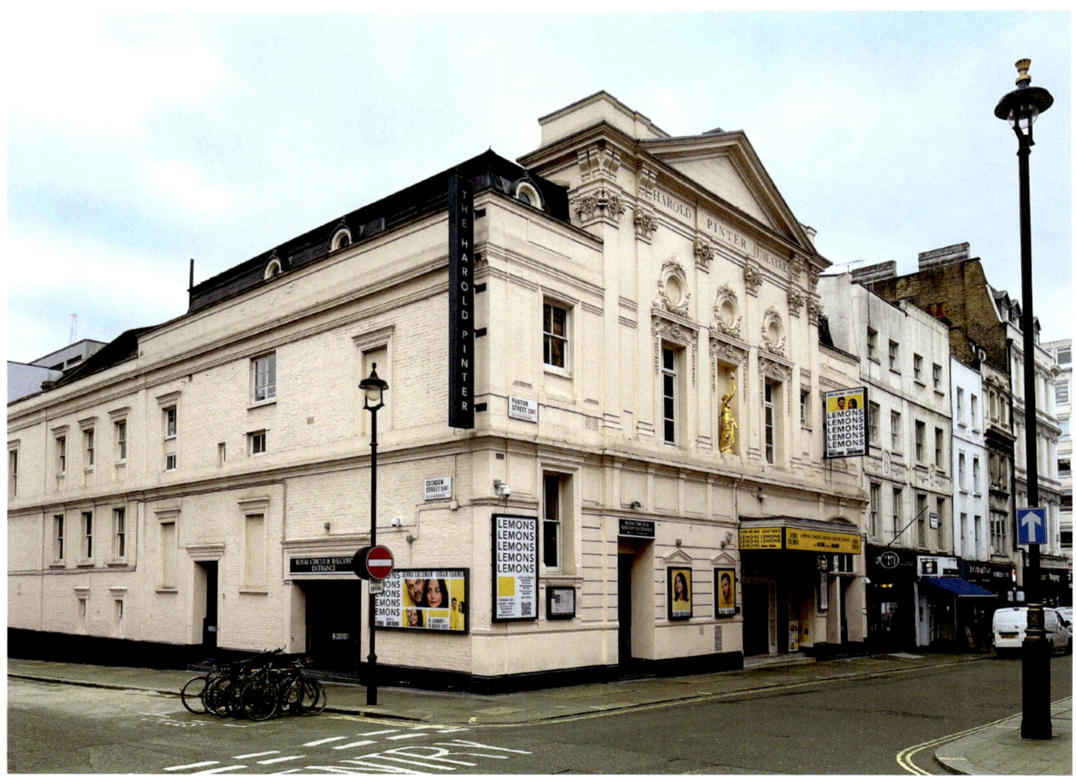

Harold Pinter Theatre, Panton Street.

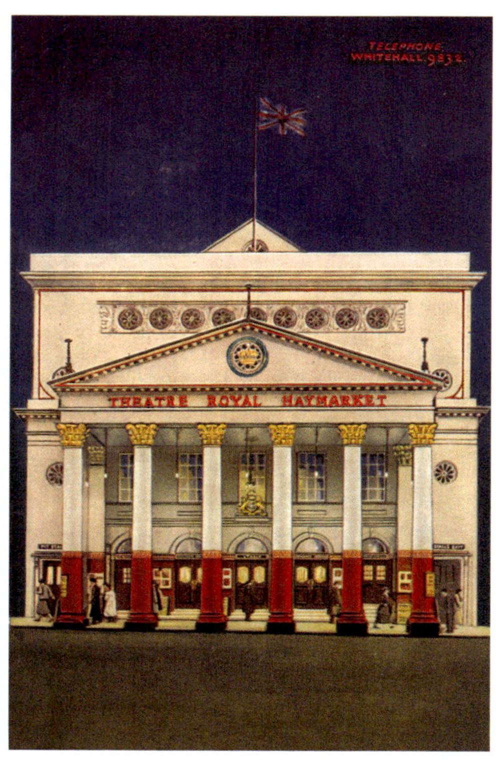

Early 1900s postcard of the Theatre Royal, Haymarket.

To the west, the Haymarket extends north to Piccadilly Circus and south to Pall Mall, said to take its name from a market selling hay and straw situated close to where horses were stabled at the Royal Mews. While the Haymarket went through a programme of redevelopment a carpenter, John Potter, built an unlicensed theatre in 1720, the Haymarket Theatre, which he was only permitted to hire out to amateur companies. Later managed by Henry Fielding, who staged a series of critique productions, the theatre closed after censorship laws came into force and remained in a derelict state until reopened by Samuel Foote, who managed to flaunt licensing laws by taking money selling chocolate and coffee drinks instead of charging admission. Foote, after an accident riding a horse on stage, encouraged to do so by the Duke of York, had his leg amputated and as a way of compensation the theatre was issued a patent.

The Haymarket was the scene of a public disaster in 1794, during the opening of a Royal Command Performance when fifteen people died in a crush gaining entry.

Rebuilt in 1820 by John Nash, the theatre was positioned further south on the Haymarket, and was the first to stage a scheduled matinée performance. Remodelled inside during the 1880s, while under the management of Herbert Beerbohm Tree, two of Oscar Wilde's plays premiered at the theatre, *A Woman of No Importance* and *Ideal Husband*.

Profits made from a production that opened in 1895, *Trilby*, the name of the play's leading female character Trilby O'Ferrall, played by Dorothea Baird, who later married Henry Irving, enabled Tree, who played Svengali in the production, to build Her Majesty's Theatre opposite in 1897, on the site of a succession of earlier theatres.

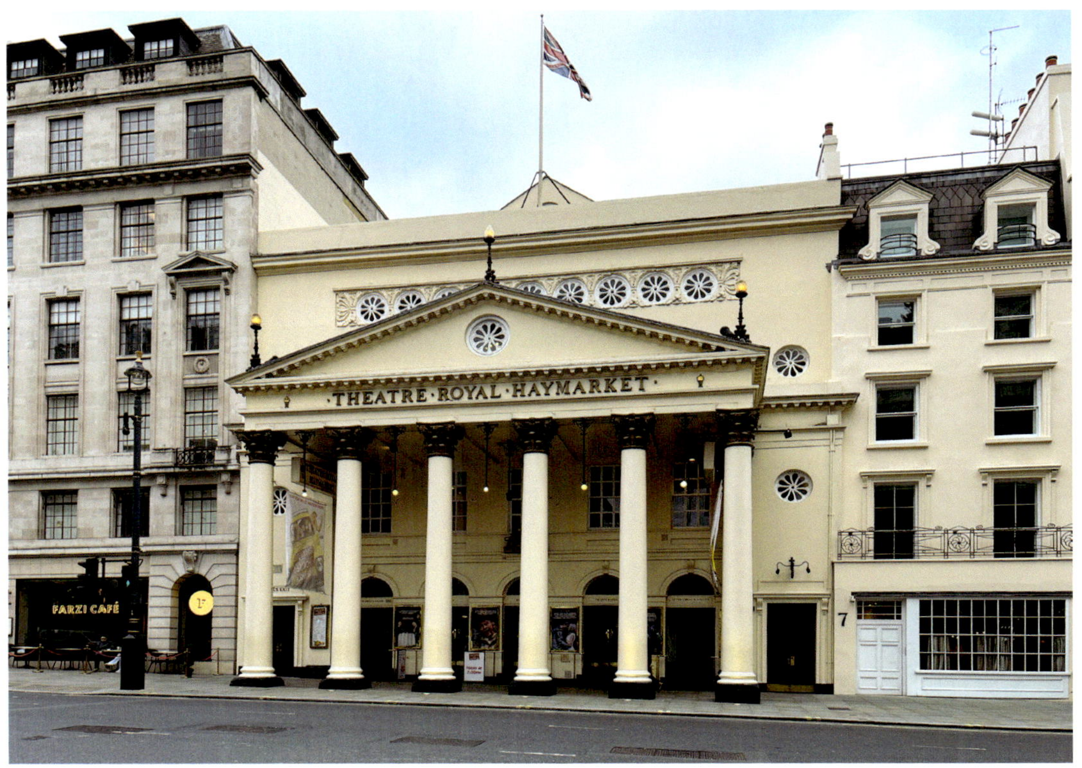

Theatre Royal, Haymarket.

The first, designed by Sir John Vanbrugh and erected in 1705, was named the Queen's Theatre, which opened with an Italian opera, *The Loves of Ergasto*. Renamed the King's Theatre ten years later, where productions were mostly operas, the theatre burned down in 1789, which was believed to have been an act of arson. Rebuilt in 1791 as an opera house by Michael Novosielski, the theatre transformed into the largest in England. Remodelled in the early 1800s and renamed Her Majesty's Theatre when Queen Victoria ascended to the throne, after a long period of success, where many leading opera stars performed including the debut in 1845 of Swedish opera singer Jenny Lind, known as the Swedish Nightingale, the theatre closed after losing custom to Covent Garden.

Although the theatre later reopened, a fire, thought to have been caused by a stove overheating, destroyed the interior of the theatre in 1867. Completely rebuilt within the theatre's shell, on completion it stood empty until 1874, when several operas were staged, including Bizet's *Carmen*, performed in England for the first time. Heavily in debt, after closing again the theatre was demolished and the site remained vacant until the present theatre, designed by C. J. Phipps in the French Renaissance style, was built along with a hotel by actor-manager Tree.

Tree founded a dramatic art school at the theatre, which became the Royal Academy of Dramatic Art, and under his ownership the theatre became a financial success, staging *Chu Chin Chow*, written, produced and directed by Oscar Asche, who also appeared in

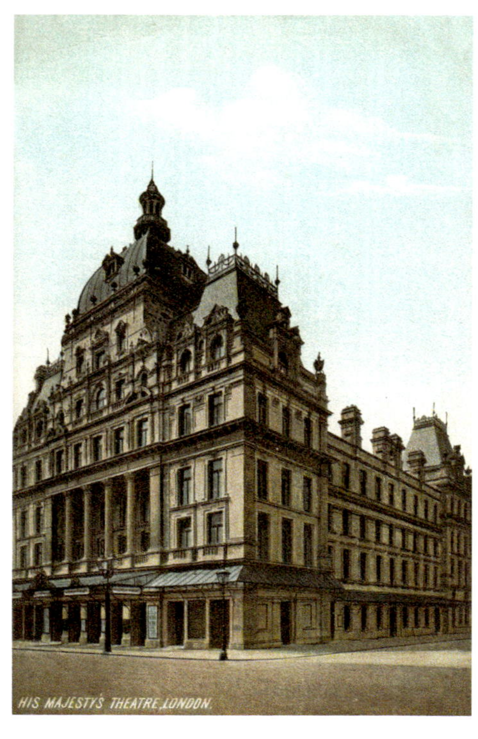

Postcard of recently built Her Majesty's Theatre, retitled His Majesty's on the death of Queen Victoria in 1901.

the musical comedy which ran for five years with 2,238 performances, a record which lasted for almost forty years. In 1986, the musical *Phantom of the Opera* premiered at Her Majesty's, starring Sarah Brightman playing soprano Christine Daaé. Brightman at the time was married to Andrew Lloyd Webber, who wrote the music for the show, with Michael Crawford playing the title role of the Phantom. During the reign of Queen Elizabeth II, the theatre was known as Her Majesty's, the name changing to His Majesty's after Charles III was crowned king.

With many new theatres going up at pace in the West End during the turn of the twentieth century, several theatres evolved off West End. Just over a mile west from the Haymarket there was an area of former marshland, once the haunt of criminals and vagabonds, where the district had been going through wholescale redevelopment after the opening of Grosvenor Canal and later Victoria main line station. The station took its name from Victoria Street, where many new properties were beginning to be erected, houses, public institutions, shops, eateries, and hotels including The Royal Standard.

Owner John Moy transformed the Royal Standard into a music hall, and after several refurbishments and rebuilds, the music hall was demolished to make way for a new theatre, under the ownership of impresario Alfred Butt, erected on the site in 1910, designed by renowned theatre architect Frank Matcham, responsible for the design of over 200 British theatres.

Opening in 1911, Victoria Palace Theatre was the last of the many great London variety houses and was exquisitely furnished throughout. The walls of the entrance hall were grey marble with adornments of gold mosaics and pillars of white Sicilian marble. The house comprised of boxes, stall, dress circle, and an upper circle, all seating just over 1,500,

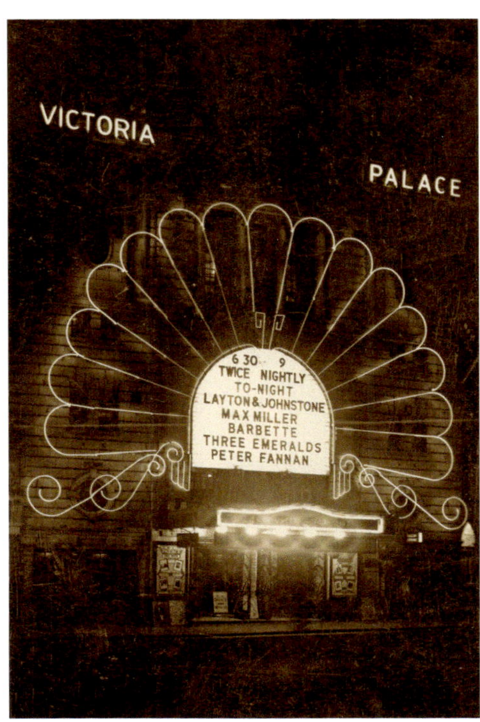

Bright lights of the Victoria Palace, 1930s.

decorated in cream with gold and deep red embellishments and curtains. Butt introduced Pavlova to London and the gold sculpture erected on top of the theatre's cupola was modelled on the ballet dancer.

One of the most successful theatres staging musicals and variety acts, including the popular comedian Max Miller, known as the Cheeky Chappie, Victoria Palace Theatre very rarely went dark, even throughout the war years, and was home to the *Crazy Gang* comedy shows and the *Black and White Minstrel* musicals, which ran for over 4,000 performances. Refurbished on several occasions, the Victoria Palace Theatre continues its reputation for staging large-scale musical productions.

A future rival of Victoria Palace Theatre was erected close by in 1929, designed by Lewis and William Edmund Trent as a super cinema with the edition of a stage, for the Gaumont chain, named the New Victoria Cinema. With two identical facades and entrances, one on Wilton Road and the other on Vauxhall Bridge Road, the building was constructed mostly in concrete, the exterior and interior designed in the art deco style. Although successful as a cinema, along with live performance theatre, there were proposals to demolish the New Victoria in the 1950s.

After closing for five years the cinema opened as a concert venue. Star performers included Joni Mitchell, Chuck Berry, Peter Gabriel, Cliff Richard, and bands such as the Kinks, Slade, and ELO.

Completely redecorated and converted into a theatre renamed Apollo Victoria, the theatre opened in September 1980, with a week of Shirley Bassey concerts. Now with a capacity of 2,328, seated over stalls, dress circle, and circle, the theatre began staging

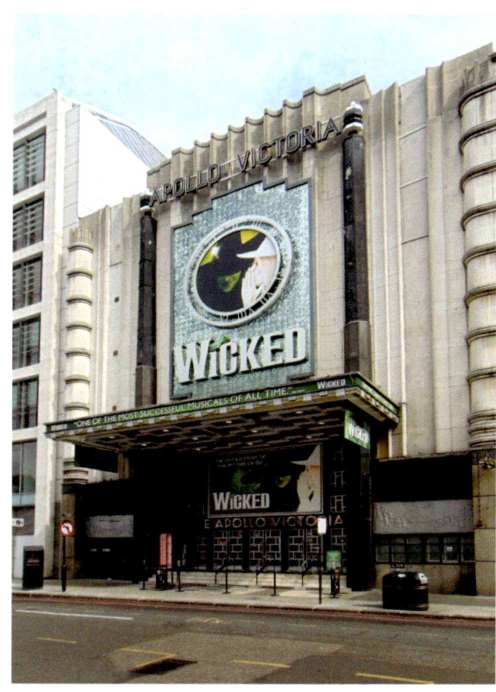

Left: Wilton Road entrance to the Victoria Apollo.

Below: The Barbican Centre housing the Barbican Theatre and The Pit.

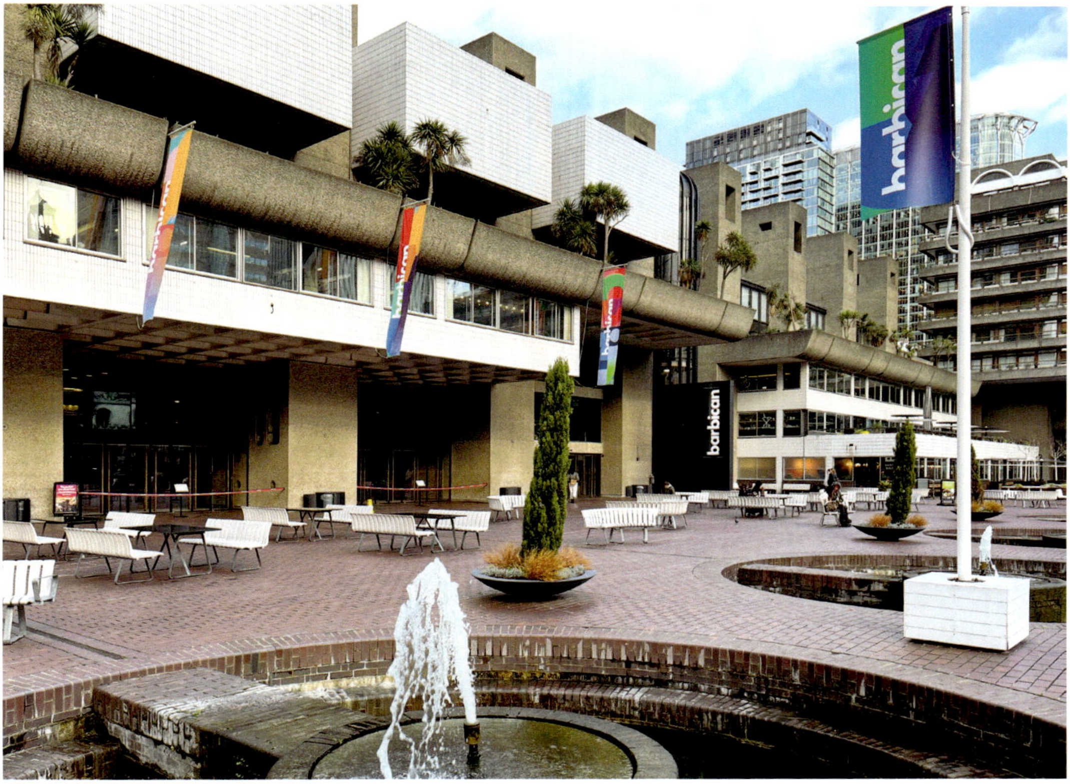

full-scale musicals. The first, *The Sound of Music*, starred Petula Clark in her musical stage debut playing Maria, with Michael Jayston as Captain Von Trapp. Other musicals that followed included Andrew Lloyd Webber and Ricard Stilgoe's *Starlight Express*, which ran for eighteen years, and more recently *Wicked*, by Stephen Schwartz, which opened in 2006.

Close to Victoria, south of Buckingham Palace, is The Other Palace Theatre, erected on the site of Westminster Theatre, which premiered with Sandi Toksvig's *Bully Boy* in 2012, and on the east side of Sloan Square is the Royal Court, a non-commercial theatre considered one of the most innovative venues for new writers and productions.

Towards the north-east of the city is the Barbican, an area devastated by bombing during the Second World War, where from the ruins a large new neighbourhood arose, incorporating tall residential properties, alongside schools, shops, and an arts and conference complex, the Barbican Centre. In 1982, the Royal Shakespeare Company took up residence at the Barbican's contemporarily designed 1,116-seat four-tier theatre, with every seat no further than 20 metres from the stage.

Performing at the Barbican Theatre up until the Shakespeare Company's contract ended in 2002, the company returned for a three-year season of Shakespeare's history plays in 2013. Along with staging classic and contemporary productions, many West End shows premiered at the Barbican, including *Les Miserables* in 1985. Within the Barbican Centre, there is also a 164-seat studio theatre, The Pit, a flexible performance space championing emerging authors, companies, and artists, and hosting a range of shows, such as *Les Liaisons Dangereuses* in 1985, starring Alan Rickman.

To the south of the city, across the Thames at Southwark, traditionally known as The Borough, after the playhouses from the time of the most well-known playwrights, Jonson, Massinger, and Shakespeare, had been demolished or fallen into disrepair, following a fire which broke out and swept through the district ten years after the Great Fire, the area fell under a long period of urbanisation. By the mid-1800s, new river crossings were constructed west of London Bridge, which opened up access along the length of the Thames from Southwark to Lambeth, and the whole district came under the administration of the new County of London in 1889.

The few older properties that remained, including coaching inns and surviving playhouses, were soon swallowed up among riverside warehouses, storehouses, and industrial buildings, while many pre-seventeenth-century structures were demolished to make way for high brick-built viaducts carrying London's new railway transport system.

The only existing theatre south of the Thames during this period, the Royal Victoria Theatre, had been erected on an undeveloped area of land, Lambeth Marsh, in 1818, to a design by Rudolph Cabanel, for founders James King, Daniel Dunn and marine painter to the king, John Serres. The foundation stone, which came from the demolished Savoy Palace on the Strand, was laid by patrons Prince Leopold of Saxe-Coburg and Princess Charlotte of Wales, the theatre named the Royal Coburg.

The grand exterior was claimed to be one of the wonderous sights of London. The theatre interior was exquisitely decorated, and included a magnificent Grand Panoramic Marine Saloon designed and executed by Serres. The Royal Coburg was a minor theatre, unable to stage serious drama; however, in 1824, under the management of George Bolwell Davidge, Edmund Kean performed in six Shakespeare plays over six nights. The audience, as described by Kean, were 'a set of ignorant, unmitigated brutes', which reflected upon the area at the time.

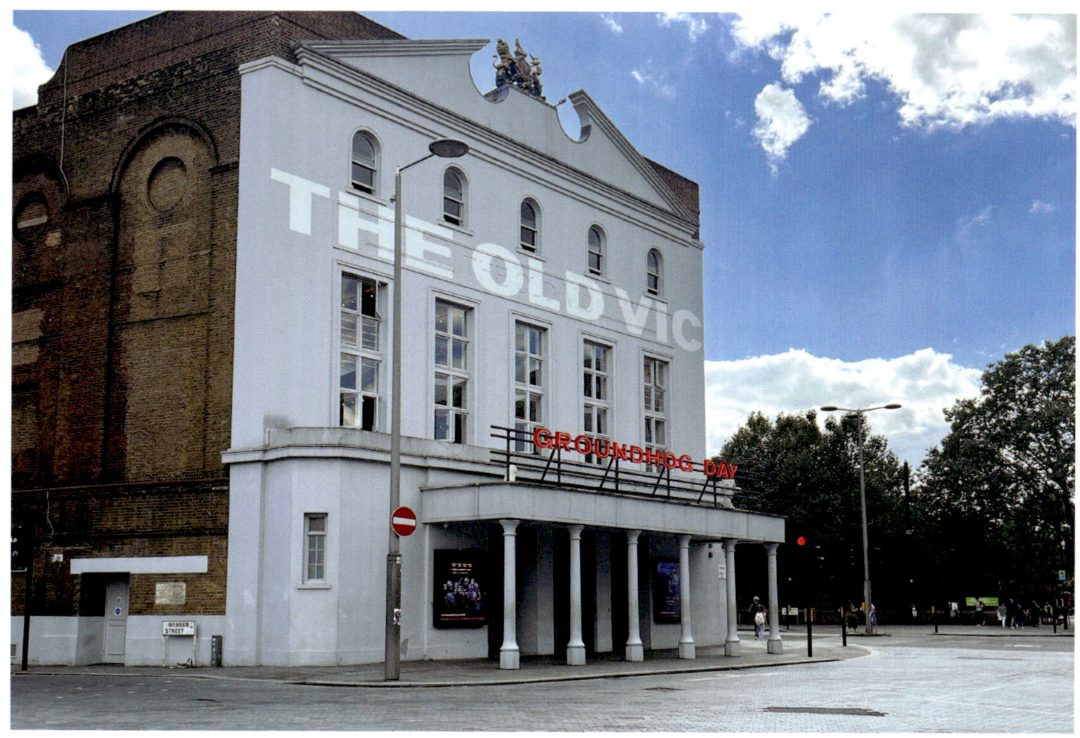

The Old Vic, on The Cut.

American-born black actor Ira Aldridge made his second appearance on the London stage at the theatre in 1833, in the production *Oroonoko*, a work of prose recalling the life of an African slave. Published in 1688, the author of *Oroonoko*, English poet and playwright Aphra Behn, is considered the first known professional female writer of her time.

Born in 1807, Aldridge grew up in New York and trained as an actor, joining the African Company, before racist attacks resulted in his emigration to Britain. Recognised as the first professional black actor to perform in London classical theatre productions, Aldridge had a highly successful critically acclaimed career, performing lead roles in many Shakespeare productions, including *Hamlet, King Lear, Macbeth,* and *Othello.*

Purchased by Daniel Egerton and William Abbot in 1833, the same year that Aldridge appeared, the Royal Coburg was renamed the Royal Victoria, under the patronage of Victoria, Duchess of Kent, mother of Princess Victoria, future queen of Britain. The theatre would go through various internal refurbishments, reconstructions, and name changes, and became known more commonly as The Old Vic, staging various productions including both ballet and opera.

Sir John Gielgud established The Old Vic Company in 1929, around the same time Dame Ninette de Valois founded a ballet company at the Sadler's Wells Theatre, the companies alternating between both.

Damaged by bombing during the Second World War, The Old Vic remained closed until repaired and reopened in the early 1950s, with a series of Shakespeare plays. The Old Vic

Company was dissolved in 1963, and under the artistic direction of Sir Laurence Olivia, the National Theatre Company was founded, based at The Old Vic. After significant restoration in the late 1900s, The Old Vic converted to a production theatre, rather than a receiving theatre, and became a remarkably successful venture under American actor Kevin Spacey, who was appointed artistic director in 2003, a position he held for fourteen years.

The current Sadler's Wells Theatre is the sixth built on the site at Islington, originating as a spar and pleasure garden in the late 1600s, where people coming for the waters were entertained by musicians and acrobats. Falling into decline during the early 1700s, considered a place of debauchery frequented by people of disrepute, the wooden-built music house was rebuilt as a theatre by John Warren. After the lease was acquired by Thomas Rosoman and Peter Hough, the theatre was reconstructed in the mid-1700s, Rosoman engaging a company of actors and dancers from Drury Lane to perform. From then onwards Sadler's Wells flourished as a minor theatre. Refurbished in the early nineteenth century, large water tanks were added for spectacular nautical productions, and by the mid-1800s, Sadler's Wells began staging serious drama.

The current theatre, designed by RHWL Architects, incorporated the frame of the previous fifth theatre and reclaimed bricks used in the new construction. With a larger sprung stage and a seating capacity of 1,500, Sadler Well's reopened in 1998 with a performance of *Iolanthe* by the Rambert Dance Company.

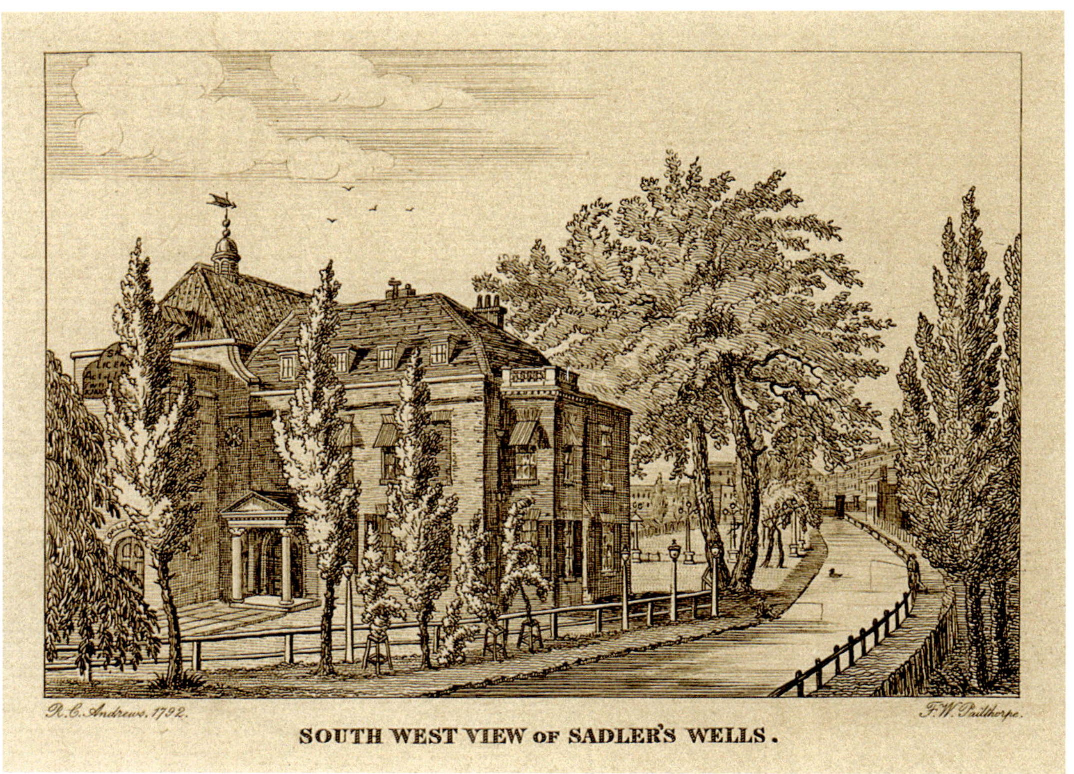

Sadler's Wells Theatre, Islington, late eighteenth century. (Wellcome Collection)

After vacating The Old Vic in 1977, the National Theatre Company moved a short distance from the Cut, near Waterloo, to the south bank of the River Thames, east of Waterloo Bridge, to take up residence at the newly built Royal National Theatre.

The demands within the theatre world to establish a national theatre were first proposed in the mid-1800s, as a London-based permanent memorial to Shakespeare and centre of dramatic education.

In the early-1900s, as part of a campaign to establish a national theatre, George Bernard Shaw wrote *The Dark Lady of the Sonnets*, a comedy where Shakespeare attempts to persuade Queen Elizabeth to create a national theatre to stage his plays. Eventually, during the mid-1900s, London County Council recommended a site close to a concert and entertainment centre, the Royal Festival Hall. The foundation stone was laid in 1951.

Usually known as the National, the publicly funded performing arts centre, a huge concrete brutalist-style complex, was designed by prominent architects Sir Denys Louis Lasdun and Peter Softley. The design divided architectural opinion at the time and continues to divide opinion today – people either love it or hate it.

Along with the 1,160-seat Olivier Theatre, the complex also accommodates the 890-seat Lyttelton Theatre, named after the National Theatre's first board chairman, government minister Oliver Lyttelton, and the Dorfman Theatre with a seating capacity of 400, named after philanthropist Lloyd Dorfman.

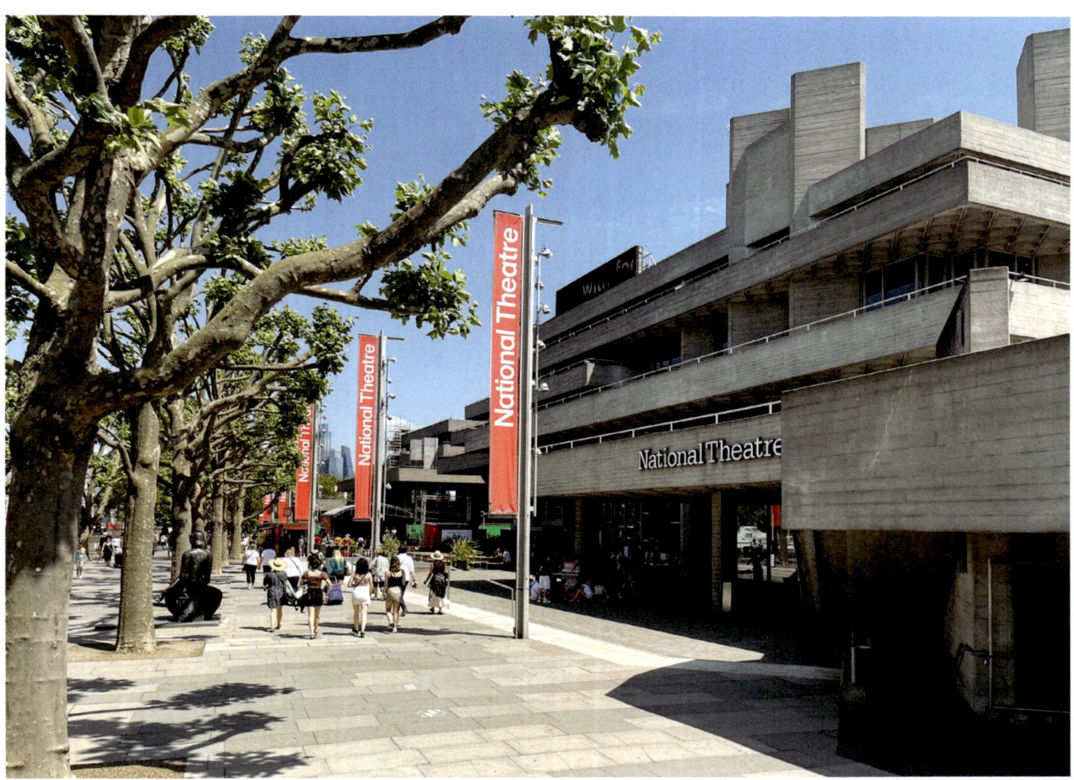

National Theatre, London's Southbank.

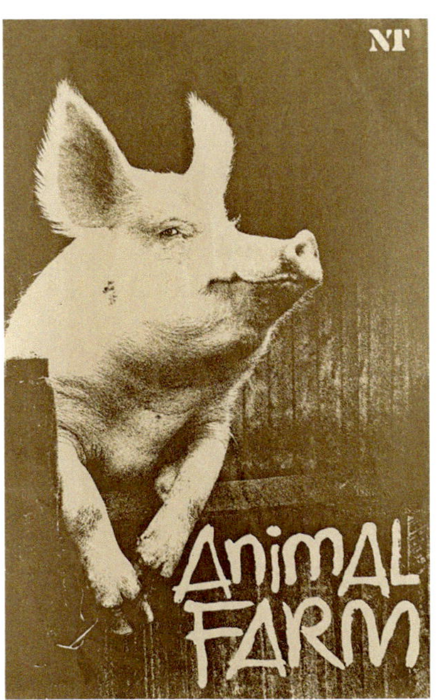

Programme from the National Theatre's production of George Orwell's chilling but timeless classic *Animal Farm*, 1984.

Backstage, the dressing rooms were constructed with windows facing each other where on the opening and closing night of a production, there is a tradition where performers drum on the glass with their hands when called to take up opening positions, known as 'beginners'.

The forecourt of the National facing the river has also been used as an entertainment and performance space for community-led events and festivals.

To the east of the Southbank, past Blackfriars Bridge and close to London Bridge, stands Shakespeare's Globe, a reconstruction based on the original Elizabethan playhouse. The new Globe was founded by American actor Sam Wanamaker, who relocated to Britain during the McCarthy witch-hunt era, a period in American history when many American actors and writers were persecuted for assumed left-wing Communist views.

Erected close to the site of the original Globe, the theatre holds 1,400, seated and standing, less than half the number of the original playhouse due to modern-day safety regulations. However, apart from the capacity of the structure, based on research by historical advisor John Orrell, Shakespeare's Globe is a faithful replica of the 1599 playhouse. Designed by architect Theo Crosby, engineering consultants Buro Happold and quantity surveyors Boyden & Co., the Globe's construction was undertaken by McCurdy & Co., using traditional materials and building methods.

Adjoining the playhouse is the actors' backstage area, contemporary designed box office, lobby, restaurant, shop, visitor centre, rehearsal studio, and education complex at embankment level, along with the adjacent Swan at the Globe, a modern riverside bar and restaurant.

Opened by Queen Elizabeth II in June 1997, although the first official public performance was *Henry V*, the king played by Mark Rylance, the Globe's first artistic director, while

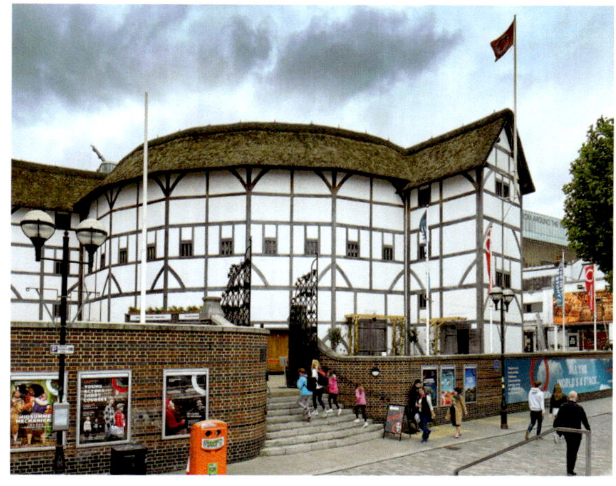

Shakespeare's Globe, Bankside.

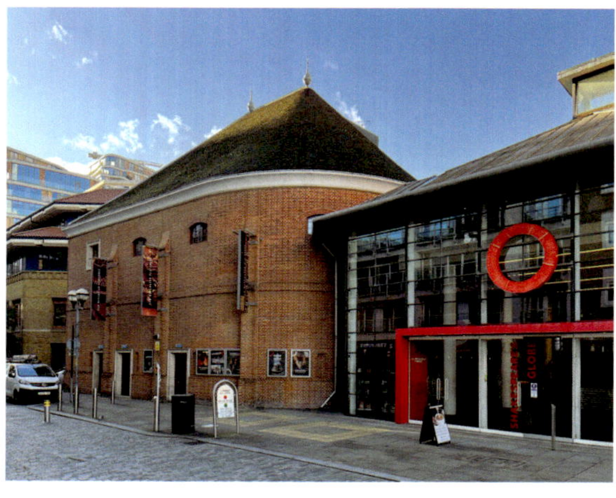

Sam Wanamaker Jacobean Playhouse, New Globe Walk.

under construction *The Merry Wives of Windsor* was performed in German by the Bremer Shakespeare Company in 1993, the same year in which Sam Wanamaker died. Not only did Wannamaker's legacy live on with Shakespeare's Globe, in 2014, an indoor Jacobean-style theatre opened adjoining the main site, named the Sam Wanamaker Playhouse, modelled on seventeenth-century Jacobean theatre plans similar in layout to Blackfriars Theatre, which once occupied a site on the opposite side of the Thames.

Designed by Jon Greenfield in collaboration with architects and urban and historical planning consultants Allies & Morrison, the playhouse, like the Globe, was constructed with traditional materials and building techniques, and apart from modern safety light features, during performances the house, with a seating capacity of 340, is lit entirely by beeswax candles mounted on sconces and height-adjustable chandeliers. The two opening productions, John Webster's *The Duchess of Malfi*, followed by Francis Beaumont's *The Knight of the Burning Pestle*, were plays first staged at Blackfriars Theatre during the early seventeenth century, plays from London's theatrical past performed in historical surroundings of the modern age.

5

Theatrical Spaces

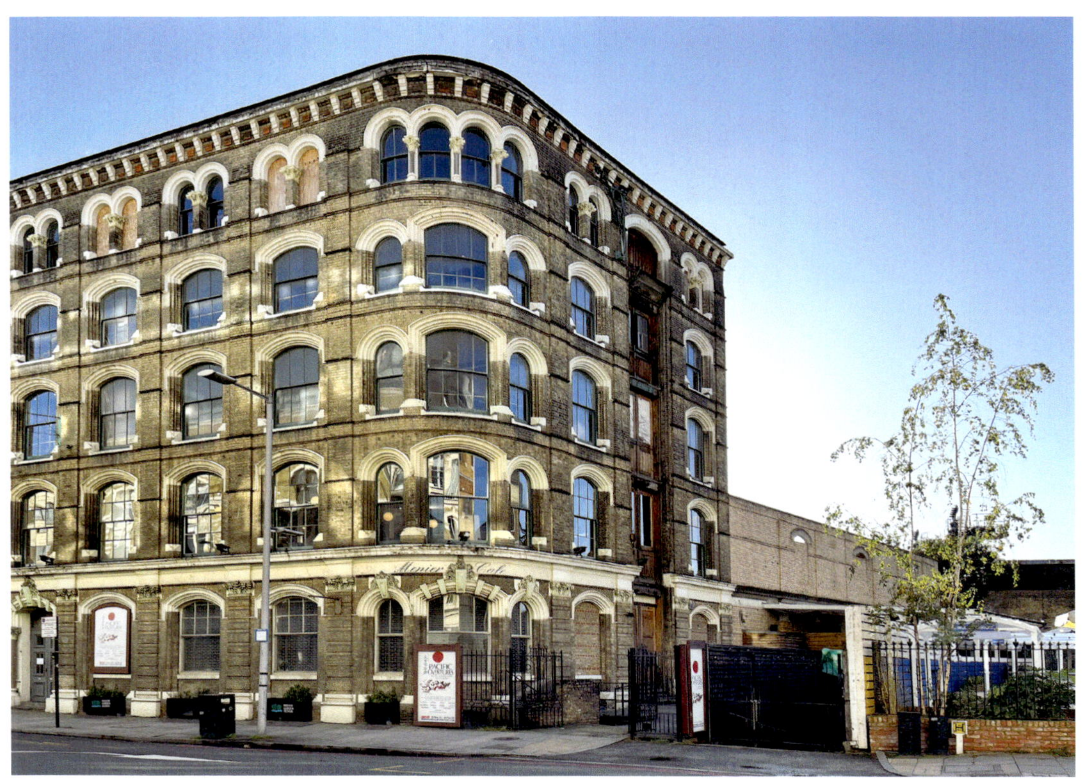

Menier Chocolate Factory, Southwark Street.

A few of London's smaller, more unusual, theatrical venues and fringe theatres occupy various buildings and repurposed properties, such as the Menier Chocolate Factory, which opened in 2004, located within a former late nineteenth-century chocolate manufacturing works, the refurbished building situated on Southwark Street; and the Jermyn Street Theatre, located in the former cellar of the Kent & Sussex Tavern, which in turn was later used as changing rooms for staff of the Spaghetti House Restaurant. The cellar was transformed into a seventy-seat theatre space under the supervision of successful entrepreneur Howard Jameson and general manager Penny Horner in 1994.

To the north of London is the re-established Victorian theatre within Alexandra Palace, once used as a storage space by the BBC, and another restored theatre can be discovered within a Grade II listed former seventeenth-century alehouse in Shadwell, Wilton's Music Hall, where entertainers such as singer and songwriter George Ware once performed, and comedian Arthur Lloyd trod the boards. Other theatres include the Almeida, a production house in Islington; Bloomsbury Theatre owned by University College London; the Old Debating Chamber within London's former County Hall; Regent's Park Open Air Theatre; and Dock X, a multi-use warehouse at Canada Water.

In the district of Soho, a small theatre company founded in 1969 by novelist and theatre director Verity Bargate and partner, theatre director, Fred Proud, relocated from The Cockpit Theatre in Marylebone to the purpose-built 165-seat Soho Theatre on Dean Street in 2000, the building housing a studio and cabaret space upstairs, and the Soho Theatre Bar

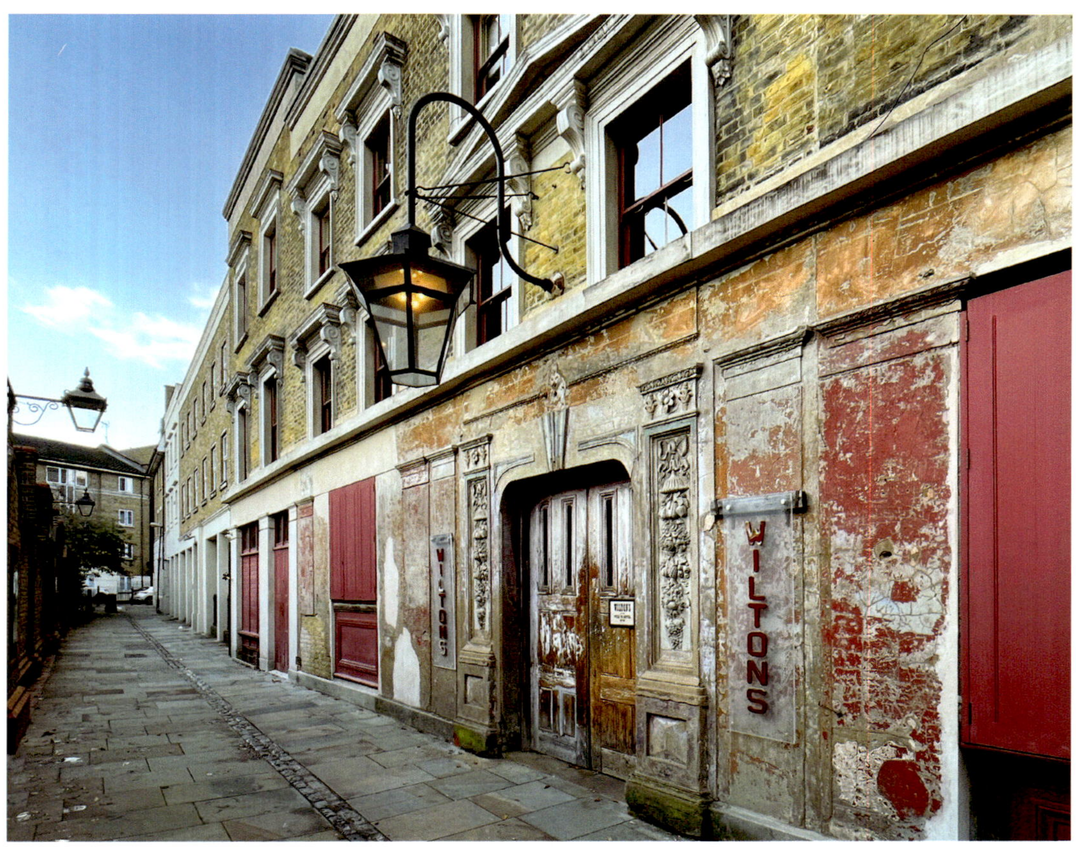

Wilton's Music Hall, Shadwell.

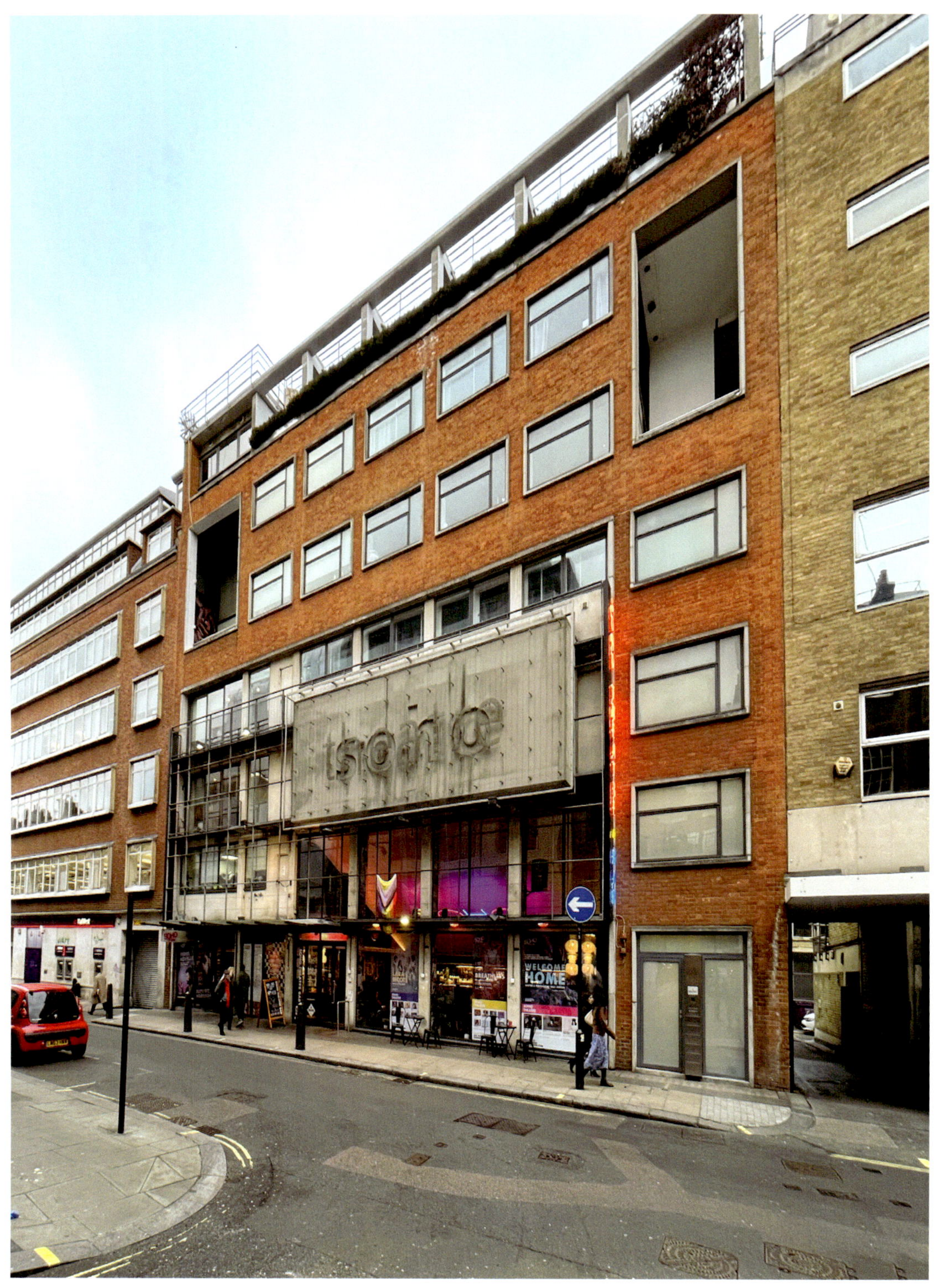

Soho Theatre, Dean Street.

on the lower two levels. A majority of productions feature new works by both promising and established playwrights, performed by emerging young actors.

One of London's more modern and innovative commercial theatrical venues is the Bridge, south of the Thames adjacent to Tower Bridge. With a capacity of 900, the stall seating can be removed when required for standing, giving audiences an immersive and, occasionally, interactive experience with the performers. The Bridge, developed by Nick Star and Nicholas Hytner, is home to the London Theatre Company. Several hit shows have been staged at the Bridge, including a revival of one of the greatest musicals of all time, *Guys and Dolls*, which opened in 2023.

Another theatre that can also be reconfigured depending on the layout of each production is the Young Vic, which evolved through near neighbour The Old Vic when the Young Vic Company was formed at the end of the Second World War. A branch of The Old Vic Theatre School performing classic plays to young audiences, although the company was later disbanded, theatre director Frank Dunlop then founded the Young Vic Theatre, and in 1970, a breeze block-built theatre was erected on a vacant bombsite on The Cut east of The Old Vic, which incorporated an adjacent former butcher's shop refurbished as the box office.

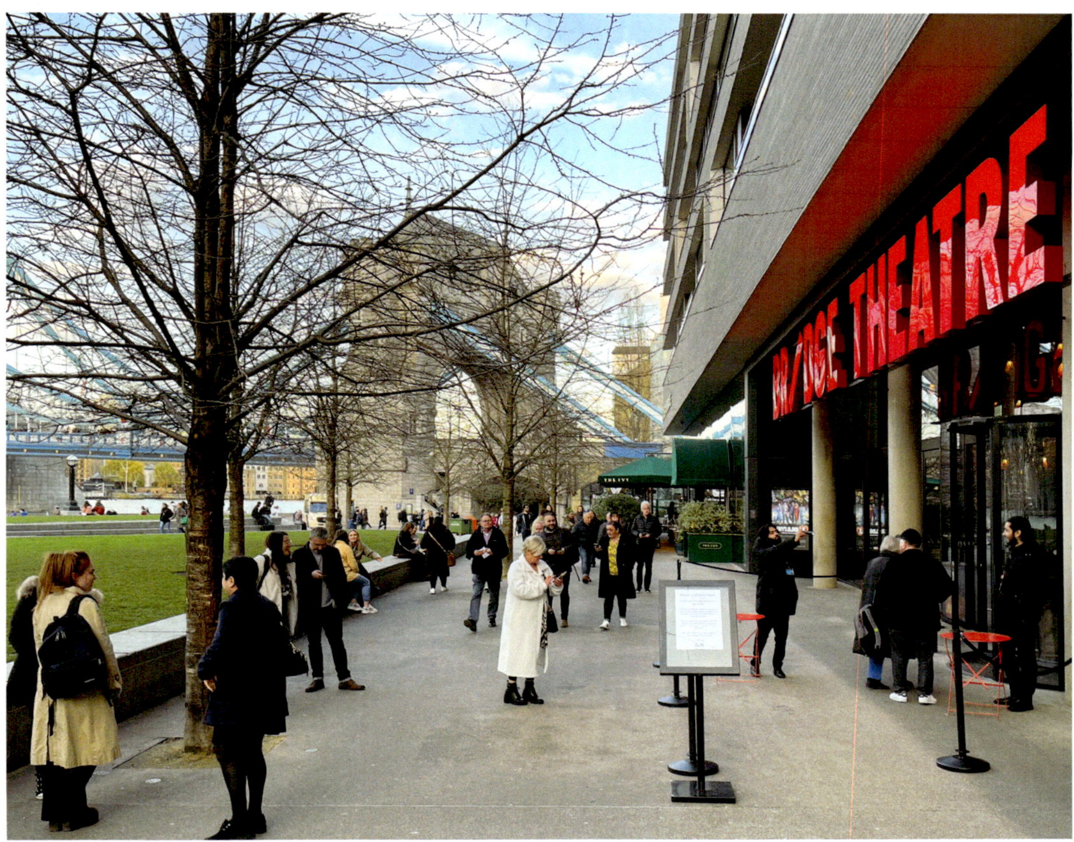

Bridge Theatre, Potters Fields Park.

The Young Vic Theatre underwent a significant rebuild and on completion, the main stage opened with a community opera production, *Tobias and the Angel* by Johnathan Dove. Two smaller theatre spaces were included within the building structure: The Clare, named after former artistic director Clare Venables, and The Maria, after theatre designer Maria Björnson.

With a long, celebrated history and fascinating heritage, London's theatres, in their all-embracing and expansive forms, are considered to be the most creative and most dazzling ever known. The patronage and support from theatregoers is the life force keeping the heart of London's theatreland beating and moving onward to an even more spectacular, bright and innovative future.

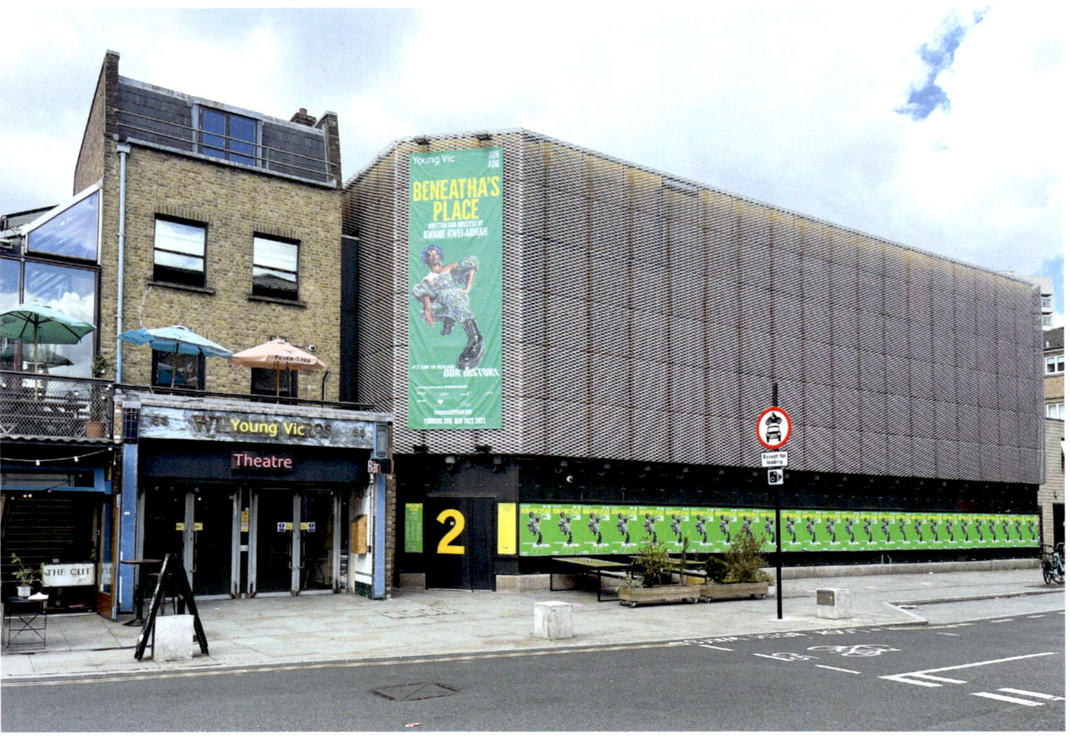

Young Vic, to the east of The Cut.

Bibliography

Books

Banham, Martin (ed.), *The Cambridge Guide to Theatre* (Cambridge, 1998)
Besant, Sir Walter, *Early London, Prehistoric, Roman, Saxon and Norman* (Adam & Charles Black, 1908)
Bostock, E. H., *Menageries, Circuses and Theatres* (Chapman & Hall, 1927)
Leapman, Michael, *Eye Witness Travel Guides – London* (Dorling Kindersley, 2000)
Lee, Sir Sidney, *A Life of William Shakespeare* (The Macmillan Company, 1916)
McNay, Walter L., *Old London* (Alexander Morning 1910)
Mander, Raymond, and Mitchenson, Joe, *The Theatres of London* (Rupert Hart-Davis, 1961)
Plimmer, Charlotte and Denis, *London A Visitor's Companion* (B. T. Batsford Ltd, 1977)
Weinreb, Ben, and Hibbert, Christopher (eds.), *The London Encyclopaedia* (Pan MacMillan, 1983)

Websites

British History Online
Historic-UK
London Theatre
London Theatres
National Archives
Old Maps Online
Victoria & Albert Museum
Victorian Web
Vision of Britain
The Wellcome Collection

Acknowledgements

The author and publisher would like to thank the following for their assistance in research for this publication, along with many theatre visits: Jennie Adams, Geoffrey Billingsley, Dean Edwards, Karen Link, Wendy Loftus, Jayne Shakeshaft, the Wellcome Collection for information and use of images on pages 6, 16, 20, 22, 26, 28, 31 and 85, and the sellers and retailers at postcard fairs and antiquarian shops who have assisted in locating images and photographs. If for any reason I have not accredited people or organisations as necessary, or used copyright material without permission/acknowledgement, I apologise for any oversight and will make the necessary correction at the first opportunity.

About the Author

Born in Greenwich, London, David Ramzan has always had a keen interest in the history of his hometown and studied local history as an undergraduate at the University of Oxford. A self-employed graphic designer, illustrator, and artist, he also worked in Special Educational Needs and has written several historical publications and articles for magazines and periodicals, subjects which include local history, maritime and football history, piracy, smuggling, and Victorian crime.